# TRAVELS WITH ALICE

# CALVIN TRILLIN

# TRAVELS WITH ALICE

AVON BOOKS ◆ NEW YORK

Portions of this work originally appeared in different form in *The New Yorker*, *Travel and Leisure*, *House and Garden*, *Saturday Night* and *Tropic*, the Sunday magazine of *The Miami Herald*.


AVON BOOKS
A division of
The Hearst Corporation
105 Madison Avenue
New York, New York 10016

The Ticknor & Fields edition contains the following Library of Congress Cataloging in Publication Data:

Trillin, Calvin.
   Travels with Alice / Calvin Trillin.
   p.  cm.
   1. Dinners and dining.  2. Voyages and travels—1981-
I. Title.
TX737.T75   1989   89-32735
641'.01'3—dc20   CIP

First Avon Books Trade Printing: November 1990

AVON TRADEMARK REG. U.S. PAT. OFF. AND IN OTHER COUNTRIES, MARCA REGISTRADA, HECHO EN U.S.A.

Printed in the U.S.A.

OPM   10  9  8  7  6  5  4  3  2  1

To some families we've been traveling with for many years — the Jowells (Jeffrey, Francie, Josie, and Danny), the Mackintoshes (Tony, Mary, Sonya, and Gabriel), and the Smiths (Bill, Genny, and, of course, Caroline T.)

# Contents

# TRAVELS WITH ALICE

# 1

## Travels with Sukey

I MIGHT HAVE SEEN more of America when I was a child if I hadn't had to spend so much of my time protecting my half of the back seat from incursions by my sister, Sukey. In the years just after the Second World War, when Sukey and I happened to be at our most territorial, our family was out on the road for five or six weeks every summer. At the time, my father was still in the grocery business, getting up before dawn six days a week so he could begin a long day by picking out his produce at the city market. For several weeks every summer, though, he entrusted even that task to others; he had decided it was important for us to see the country. Living in Kansas City, we were, as the real estate people might put it, equally convenient to either coast — not to speak of the Gulf of Mexico, which was only nine hundred miles or so to the south. We usually headed west, toward the Pacific, making our way across the Southwest on Route 66 or cutting up to British Columbia from Highway 40 and then following the coastline down to California. At some point we'd come to rest for a couple of weeks near the beach in Santa Monica, in what was then called a tourist court. Whichever route we took, we seemed to pass a lot of mesas. Also buttes. If I hadn't had a sister with an expansionist back-seat policy, I would probably now know the difference between a mesa and a butte.

There were a lot of roadside zoos — places that began advertising miles in advance that they offered a unique opportunity to see an albino raccoon or a two-headed goat or the world's smallest sheep dog. I could never understand why my father wasn't willing to stop at every single roadside zoo in the West. Even now I can't explain it. I realize, of course, that the zoos were come-ons for filling stations or maybe even flimflam dice games, but I still can't imagine passing up an opportunity to see an albino raccoon. Also, the stops were about the only time I could concentrate on what I was supposed to be seeing, relieved temporarily from the tension of maintaining a full border alert in the back seat.

At the end of the day we always knew how many

miles we had driven. It was of only academic interest to us; we never had any reservations or any particular time we had to be anywhere. Still, we took
some pride in covering ground. When I got old
enough to travel with friends, we concentrated on
making time as if we were trying to beat a rival ex-
pedition to the Pole. The summer I got out of high
school, I drove with two friends to the Minnesota
lake country for a canoe trip, and even on the way
home we waited until red lights to change drivers so
as not to waste any time — although I can't think of
much we were doing with our time in Kansas City
that summer beyond going down to LeRoy's Tavern
to talk dirty.

I later found out that the English, who don't have
nearly as much ground to cover, tend to view the
American approach to highway travel as somewhere
between baffling and pathological. A couple of years
after I got out of college, some English friends of
mine were given a ride from northern Spain to Paris
by an American we all knew, and to their astonish-
ment he drove straight through without stopping.
They came to the conclusion that he was suffering
from a latent death wish. I informed them that our
mutual friend had merely driven from northern
Spain to Paris the way any red-blooded American
boy would drive from northern Spain to Paris: he
made good time.

Growing up tends not to cure Americans of the notion that the number of miles covered is an important gauge to the success of pleasure travel. In fact, the American tour industry operates on the assumption that it is dealing with people in a hurry. The way tourism is now organized in America, it is assumed that travelers who want to see some calves roped and some broncos busted while in the West will take advantage of some efficiently packaged place with a name like RodeoLand USA, or maybe Cowboy Country. (Actually, it wouldn't be surprising to find RodeoLand USA in New Jersey — a Western wonderland plopped into the Jersey swamps to take advantage of what I sometimes call the Doctrine of Creative Inappropriateness. The Doctrine is based on the theory that tourists will stop in an ersatz Alpine town in Georgia not simply because they think it might be years before they get to Switzerland itself but because they treasure the notion of the gift shop clerk saying something like "I'm fixin' to show y'all some real nice *Lederhosen*.")

Making good time through, say, Texas, the potential visitors to RodeoLand USA figure that if they luck into an uncrowded Burger King for lunch they might make Albuquerque by dark and have a five-hundred-mile day under their belts. The kids want to see a rodeo, but not at the cost of having to sit in a broken-down grandstand for a couple of hours

knowing that each minute is a minute more they'll
have to wait before hitting the pool at the Albuquerque Best Western. RodeoLand USA will offer them
two or three representative rodeo events in a modern grandstand. There will be a multimedia exhibit
on rodeo history and a room devoted to one of the
four largest collections of barbed wire in the world.
Several legendary broncos and wild bulls will be displayed, stuffed, in action poses. There might be a
mechanical bronco for the braver kids to try out.
There will be clean and well-maintained rest rooms.
There will be a gift shop that has souvenir T-shirts
and lassos and RodeoLand USA ashtrays and Rodeo-
Land USA beer caddies and some coffee mugs in-
scribed with cow-chip jokes. There will be snack
bars, featuring the Buckin' Bullburger. All of this,
not counting the souvenirs and the bullburgers, will
be included in a single "family special" one-shot admission charge. The entire visit will be over in forty-
five minutes. Cowboys will have been seen. Albuquerque will be reached before dark.

My wife, Alice, and I happened to be out West in
the summer of 1971; our first daughter, Abigail,
who was then two years old, was with us. I had a
couple of weeks' work to do in Gallup, New Mexico,
a trading town on the edge of the Navajo reservation, and we found a Holiday Inn with a large en-
closed grassy area and a little playground. As we

were getting Abigail some dinner in the motel dining room on the second evening of our stay, the waitress said, "Car break down?" I didn't understand the question until I realized that she had never seen a family stay more than one night. It was at that moment that I realized something essential about American travel: Americans drive across the country as if someone's chasing them. They tend to move across Europe at the same pace. Traveling in Europe, some of them may give up counting miles and start counting cathedrals, or even countries. For anyone who has ever made good time on Interstate 70, there aren't enough miles in Europe to make any difference.

While we were in Gallup we drove out to a ramshackle little arena on the Navajo reservation for a rodeo that was nothing like the one at RodeoLand USA. Rodeos, like pickup trucks and country-and-western music, have been folded into Navajo culture. The contestants were tough, wiry Navajo cowboys. The crowd in the grandstand was distinguished by a number of traditionally dressed Navajo women, each of whom seemed to be wearing the price of a string of rodeo ponies in silver around her neck. We had found out about the rodeo through an advertisement taped in a drugstore window in Gallup. On a stroll down the main street in any town, we often stop to read notices taped in a drugstore window, just on the off chance that we happen to have hit town on the very evening that the volunteer fire department is holding the annual hog roast that has become a legend throughout that entire end of the state. I suppose you could say that we're not usually in much of a hurry. For a long time I didn't know any other way of explaining how the sort of pleasure traveling we do differs from the sort that amounts to being chased down the interstate, but several years ago I finally realized that we spend a lot of time in activities that the LeRoy's Tavern crowd would call hanging around.

Some people who thrive on the bright lights and the certified sights might say that as travelers we are just easily entertained. I can't deny that I get pretty excited if I learn that, by extraordinary chance, the very weekend we happen to be in some fishing town on Chesapeake Bay is the day of the annual oyster roast. In fact, I'd be pretty excited to find out that Wednesday, the day we happen to be in some provincial city in Mexico, is the day local farmers bring their produce to the town square — and if it turns out that they come on Thursday, we're very likely to stay over. Given an extra afternoon, we could always visit the little church that got to look sort of interesting the sixth or seventh time we passed it, or we could always take another stroll down a street whose shops showed some indication of constituting the broken hardware district. If we're looking at a window display of broken hardware the second time, it wouldn't be surprising if the proprietor, in a friendly sort of way, said, "Car break down?"

Actually, our car did break down once, in a lovely coastal town called Elk, California. This was when Abigail and her younger sister, Sarah, were teenagers. We've never had a nicer day anywhere — partly, I think, because there was no question of moving on. I was reminded of a time, just before Abigail was born, when Alice and I found ourselves with a one-week enforced stay in the Kingdom of Tonga because of a fortuitous mechanical problem in what was then Air Polynesia's entire fleet of plane. The Kingdom of Tonga, which sometimes billed itself as the Friendly Islands, turned out to be an exception to the general rule that a comfortable hotel becomes economically feasible in an island paradise when the number of tourists increases to the point at which the island is no longer a paradise. A couple of years before, in anticipation of the important international visitors expected for the coronation of King Taufaahau Tupou IV, the capital city of Nukualofa had acquired a hotel of the sort that would ordinarily not have been expected until there were enough tourists to support four or five boutiques and a Hertz agency. As a sort of bonus, the most splendid public functions of the kingdom were held in the hotel's outdoor dining room, so that the few overnight guests became included merely by showing up for dinner — a policy that permitted us to be present at the Miss Nukualofa contest, won by a young woman who was sponsored by a local bakery and entered as Miss Friendly Island Biscuits.

Some cities, of course, seem almost designed for hanging around. I think of Lucca, in northern Tuscany, that way. The central part of the city is surrounded by a wall, a proper brick rampart built in the sixteenth and seventeenth centuries by people who, though they might have heard a lot of nice things about the Florentines, still held to the old maxim that good fences make good neighbors. The wall is thick enough to provide a shaded thoroughfare on top for people interested in literally taking a walk around town. Within the wall, automobile traffic is limited and, in a core of narrow, meandering streets, nonexistent. People have favorite bits of Luccan architecture — a particular Romanesque church, a red-brick tower, a courtyard that turns out to be an ancient amphitheater. I'm partial myself to the church of San Michele, whose front wall has two elaborate extra floors extending above the roof, as if the architect were a baker who so loved making decorative icing that he continued even after he had run out of cake. But for people with a predilection for hanging around, the best thing about central Lucca is the way the place is put together. At six or seven in the evening, the entire city seems to be out on a stroll, stopping here and there to chat with a friend or buy a loaf of bread or inspect a shop window. Lucca is, I think, what Americans on their way to Italy have in mind when they try to envision what Florence must be like — minus the sort of art Florence has, of course, although there are those who would argue that Lucca's best-known product is what would have resulted if a multi-talented man like Michelangelo had turned his hand to the manufacture of olive oil.

On the other hand, we've hung around happily in Tokyo and on small Caribbean islands. At some point I figured out what my father might have known all along about family travel: it doesn't make a tremendous amount of difference where you go. As long as a family has escaped in a pack from the preoccupations of home, a tourist court in Santa Monica is not that different from a house in Provence. I don't mean that we haven't spent a lot of time selecting destinations. After we had begun taking the girls along on trips, during what I always thought of as the window of opportunity — that period when children are old enough to travel with their parents comfortably but not old enough to have better things to do — we had criteria that moved over the years from the availability of disposable diapers (Tonga, as we remembered it, had not struck us as the sort of place that might be strong in that category) to the proximity of beaches. When Alice and I took a trip by ourselves, our choice was affected by what I'm afraid is a weakness on Alice's part for romantic spots with views — a weakness I have always attributed to the fact that Alice, having been an only child in a family not given to long summer car trips, was deprived of the opportunity to learn that travel is less about romance than about protecting your side of the back seat.

Alice and I and the girls never took the same sort of car trip that I used to take with my parents and Sukey. We talked about it now and then, but it never worked out. Living in New York, of course, meant that we were not equally convenient to either coast, and as a loyal son of the plains I always winced when Alice suggested that we simply fly over the middle of the country to some place like Denver or Albuquerque and then drive through what she persisted in calling "the interesting part." I'm sorry we never got to drive across the country with the girls. It's too late now; they've got better things to do. I still think back a lot on those trips I took as a child, especially when I'm driving through some part of the country I particularly like the looks of — the

Oregon coast or the high desert of New Mexico or the plains of central Kansas, near where I grew up, where the strain of wheat they plant now comes up short and thick, like a fifties crew cut. I sometimes imagine myself at the wheel and my own girls in the back seat, in an air-conditioned car this time, but still, somehow, on Route 66. We're somewhere between Amarillo and Tucumcari, heading west. A sign along the side of the highway says JUST AHEAD: SEE ALBINO RACCOON. I put my foot on the brake.

# 2

## Defying Mrs. Tweedie

BEFORE ALICE AND I LEFT for a visit to the Sicilian resort town of Taormina, I consulted *Sunny Sicily* for the observations of Mrs. Alec Tweedie, a rather severe travel writer of late Victorian times who was also the author of *Through Finland in Carts* and, before she caught on to the value of a snappy title, *Danish Versus English Butter Making.* I can't imagine why some people say that I don't have a scholarly approach to travel.

Writing in 1904, Mrs. Tweedie summed up Taormina like this: "The place is being spoilt." It's the sort of comment that can give pause to a traveler who is considering a visit to Taormina somewhat later in the century. Mrs. Tweedie's conclusion that Taormina was being ruined by an influx of English and Americans must have been made, after all, at about the same time the Wright brothers took off at Kitty Hawk — and neither she nor the Wright brothers could have had any notion of the impact of Super-APEX fares. There was no way for me to know whether or not Mrs. Tweedie had been one of those people who simply seem to take great pleasure in telling you that they can recall the time when the place you're about to visit — any place you're about to visit — was actually O.K. ("Pity about the Marquesas. I remember thinking years ago that if that semimonthly prop service from Fiji ever started, that would be it.")

Still, even though Mrs. Tweedie complained bitterly that "the natives have lost their own nice ways," she had to admit that Taormina was "one of the most beautiful spots on earth," an ancient town perched high on a mountain overlooking the Ionian Sea. Also, I had reason to believe that Mrs. Tweedie's standards in matter of spoilage were stricter than my own. She sounded as if she might fit comfortably among those travelers whose measure of authenticity is so exacting that they tend to find even the ruins ruined.

Taormina, in fact, happens to have a noted ruin — a Greek theater where what must have been the cheap seats command such a spectacular view of Mount Etna and the sea and ninety thousand bougainvillea that I can imagine Aristophanes and Euripides sitting around some playwrights' hangout commiserating with each other on how hard it is to hold a Taormina audience's attention. As a matter of fact, Mrs. Tweedie did find that ruin ruined. The Greek theater, she wrote, "is really Roman, as the Romans completely altered it." I have nothing against the Romans myself. How is it possible to dismiss a culture that handed down spaghetti carbonara? Although I don't have much interest in gazing upon volcanic mountains from afar — I find it preferable only to gazing upon them up close — I was, of course, traveling with a connoisseur of views. I always seem to be particularly intent on pleasing Alice during Italian vacations, even if that requires taking in what I would think of as a plethora of views. It may have grown out of my custom of calling her the *principessa* whenever we're traveling in Italy. At some point I found that it improved the service at the hotels.

By Mrs. Tweedie's standards, the natives of Taormina must have lost their own nice ways years before she marched briskly into the piazza, wearing, as I have always envisioned her, a tweed suit, sensible walking shoes, and an authoritative expression. At the time of Mrs. Tweedie's first inspection, the British had been coming to Taormina for thirty years, presumably attracted by an assortment of feasts for the eye — from the long view of Etna and the sea to the constant sight of flowers tumbling over the walls of medieval stone buildings to the sudden surprising slice of sea visible through an alley so narrow that the flower-bedecked balconies on either side almost meet overhead. Those are the sorts of vistas, of course, that only arouse suspicion in somebody with Mrs. Tweedie's keen eye. "Somehow the scene never looks quite real," she complained after taking in a view she found irritatingly gorgeous.

When Mrs. Tweedie was probably still skidding around Finland in a cart, Taormina already had a grand hotel: the San Domenico Palace, which was opened in 1895 in a converted sixteenth-century monastery. Apparently, a visit by Wilhelm II of Prussia made Taormina popular with all sorts of royalty, Vanderbilts and Rothschilds as well as Hohenzollerns — all the more reason to believe, it seemed to me, that the operators of the San Domenico, where we stayed, would know how to treat someone referred to incessantly by her escort as the *principessa*.

Taormina also picked up a reputation as a place that appealed to writers and artists and assorted genteel bohemians. It almost goes without saying that D. H. Lawrence once lived there. Having had D. H. Lawrence residences pointed out to me all over the world, I can only wonder how he got any writing done, what with packing and getting steamship reservations and having to look around for a decent plumber in every new spot. I suspect, though, that Taormina's reputation for harboring exotics comes less from Lawrence than from a German nobleman named Wilhelm von Gloeden, who arrived at about the same time as Wilhelm II and started taking what became well-known photographs of Sicilian boys — some dressed as ancient Greeks, some dressed as girls, and some not dressed at all.

Late in the evening, as I sat in one of the outdoor cafés on Taormina's principal piazza, where one café uses enlargements of von Gloeden photographs to decorate its walls, my thoughts sometimes turned from Sicilian almond pastry to the possibility that von Gloeden and Mrs. Tweedie met in Taormina. The street that dominates the town — the Corso Umberto, a strolling street that bans cars except during early-morning delivery hours — couldn't have changed much from the days when there were no cars to ban, except that in Mrs. Tweedie's time the industrial revolution had not progressed to the point of providing Corso Umberto shops with souvenir T-shirts that say I MAFIOSI TAORMINA. The piazza, known as Piazza Nove Aprile, is a wide spot about halfway down the Corso Umberto where a gap in the buildings along one side of the street for a few hundred feet presents a stunning view of the sea. The jacaranda trees must have been there then, and I suspect the bench alongside the sixteenth-century church was lined with the very same nineteenth-century old folks, sternly watching the evening strollers as if collecting vicarious sins to confess the next day.

I could easily imagine the encounter. Suddenly a man at one of the cafés stands up, trying to keep his composure while gathering up the bulky cameras and tripod he always carries with him. "I really don't see what concern it is of yours, madam," he says in heavily accented English.

Too late. Mrs. Tweedie is bearing down on him, brandishing the umbrella that made a porter in Palermo sorry that he complained about what had been a perfectly adequate sixpence tip. Von Gloeden bolts from the café, knocking down a portly mustachioed man (Wilhelm II of Prussia) and caroming off an ice cream vendor as he races down the street. Mrs. Tweedie is gaining on him.

"Shame! Shame!" she shouts as she waves the lethal umbrella above her head. "Shame on you, you wicked, wicked man!"

Mrs. Tweedie couldn't have been the last person to find Taormina spoiled. I suspect that Tweedie-like comments have been made about the place pretty steadily ever since. They are based partly on the belief that Taormina is a European outpost that is almost unrelated to what Lawrence Durrell called "the wild precincts of Sicily." It has always been seen as a worldly resort that, by some accident of history, happens to be on the east coast of Sicily instead of on the Riviera or the Argentario. All of that is true, of course, even though Taormina seemed stuffed full of things Sicilian — a vast variety of Sicilian ice cream and Sicilian marzipan and Sicilian pastry, weekly performances of the traditional Sicilian puppet show, an annual festival celebrating the intricately painted Sicilian horse cart, and, now and then, that bracing, life-enhancing smell of pure garlic.

It may be, though, that Taormina has survived as a resort partly because it always served as a comfortable outpost of Europe on what has traditionally been thought of as a harsh, almost North African island. The precincts of Sicily are not nearly as wild as they once were, but the tourist amenities are still spread pretty thin. A tourist traveling around the island to take in its Greek and Roman and Byzantine treasures has reason to be grateful for a place that openly specializes in what the American army used to call Rest and Rehabilitation. The person who has been doing the driving on a tour of Sicily may arrive in Taormina suffering from the sort of nervous exhaus-

tion once associated with soldiers arriving for R & R
in Tokyo from a tour as artillery spotters in Korea.
It is not true, as is often heard in Europe, that Sicilian drivers are unpredictable: they can be counted
on to pass. On the highway, Sicilians pass on
straightaways, they pass on hills, they pass on curvy
hills and hilly curves. In a large city like Palermo or
Catania or Messina, a traveler trapped in a motion-
less line of cars on a conventional two-lane street
can suddenly find himself being passed on both the
left and the right at the same time.

In Taormina there is no need to drive at all. The
layout of the town seems designed for the stroll. The
logical way to get to Mazzarò, the beach at the foot
of the mountain, is on a funicular, which can't be
passed on either side. The big decisions made by
visitors to Taormina are on the order of deciding
whether to have the grilled shrimp or the grilled
swordfish, or deciding whether to take an evening
stroll along the Corso Umberto or in the public gardens, where spaces for the benches have been cut
out of thick bushes of bougainvillea.

Some friends of ours named Tony and Mary Mackintosh had joined us in Taormina. Mary, a college
friend of Alice's, married Tony, who's English, not
long after graduation, and they've lived in England
ever since. We see them in London or in New York
or, now and then, in some third country. As travelers

we've always been compatible. They're not the sort of people who are going to push for a stroll in the Corso Umberto if you happen to feel like going to the public gardens instead — they'll just catch up with you in the café later — nor the sort of people who find it troubling that the venue of the evening stroll is the big decision of the day. Which is to say, I suppose, that they're easily entertained themselves.

It should be said that once we had made the strolling decision each evening, we did have a couple of other matters to settle. We had to select an appropriate ice cream cone for Alice, and we had to collect entries for our private marzipan contest. As it happens, Alice is even more interested in *gelato* — Italian ice cream — than she is in views. In Taormina we often spent a good part of the evening systematically checking out the various *gelaterias,* with Alice inspecting the *gelati* displays the way Mrs. Tweedie might have run her eye over a Greek façade that she suspected of having Roman alterations. Our marzipan collection had nothing to do with eating. I'm not sure I know anybody who actually likes to eat marzipan. All of us were simply so astonished at the variety of foodstuffs Sicilians can duplicate in pure marzipan — absolutely realistic bananas and oranges and figs and onions and cucumbers and lobsters — that we thought it only appropriate to give a prize for sheer imagination. For a while we figured the prize would go to a shop near the cathedral that displayed miniature provolone cheeses made of marzipan. Then, on a side street, we discovered the winner. The display consisted of a generous helping of spaghetti, including parsley and cloves of garlic, and next to that a fried egg.

I wasn't kidding myself. Even though we had taken on those additional responsibilities, Mrs. Tweedie would have accused us of frittering away our time in Taormina, relaxing in a resort when we could have been inspecting ruins or perhaps even studying the difference between Danish and English butter making. If we'd had the sort of gumption Mrs. Tweedie expected from proper tourists, we could have questioned Tony closely on how the English make butter and then picked up the Danish end on some future trip to Scandinavia.

Sitting in a café, I could sometimes imagine Mrs. Tweedie standing before me, like a stern bus-tour guide of vaguely Germanic origins who is outraged at seeing one of her charges having a quiet drink when he's supposed to be on the tour of the glass-making factory and the eighteenth-century grist mill. "This is not a free morning," she reminds me, in her voice but von Gloeden's accent.

"But Taormina has existed so long as a resort that

you can think of it as a historic site itself," I'd say to Mrs. T., edging out of umbrella range as I said it. "Even the cafés."

It's true — or true enough. For instance, a century in the business has left Taormina with a display of just about every sort of hotel that has attracted people to European resorts through changing times and fashions. Between *gelaterias*, we sometimes found ourselves touring hotels — from peaceful, old-fashioned places that conjure up a European resort of the twenties, to those sleek, hard-edged new Italian beach hotels that must retain a couple of porters to go through regularly and remove anything that looks inviting to sit on. In the first few days in Taormina, I seemed to be taking a tour of the San Domenico every time I tried to find my way back to our room — in the "new section," added to the monastery building in 1926. I would wander through courtyards thick with flowers, down high hallways decorated with an occasional icon that seemed to have been left behind by the previous owners, in and out of public rooms that by size and design appeared to have been built for basketball games between the Wilhelm II Royal Five and the Rothschild Bouncing Bankers. Apparently, a lot of people who were not paying guests wanted to take tours of the San Domenico on purpose. A sign outside said, in four languages, IT IS NOT ALLOWED TO VISIT THE HOTEL.

A resort, like an ancient theater, is altered by suc-
ceeding occupations. Despite some lingering reputation for elegance and artiness, Taormina had actually become a place that catered mainly to what its
more or less official guidebook calls "mass tourism."
The English and Americans whose presence trou-
bled Mrs. Tweedie were no longer in evidence; they
had been replaced by people on group tours from
Italy or Germany or Scandinavia. On a summer Saturday night the Corso Umberto appeared to be dominated by middle-class residents of Catania and Messina who had driven over for a day's outing, making
Taormina authentically Sicilian in a way Mrs. Tweedie could never have imagined. Although some pros-
perous Italian families may always return to the San
Domenico for the Christmas holidays, the time had
passed when Taormina was the place to observe the
sort of chic Europeans seen in resorts like Porto
Ercole or Cap Ferrat — the men in spotless white
pants and espadrilles, the women looking as if they
spend half their time at Gucci and the other half at
the gym. Like Greek details in what was eventually
converted into a Roman theater, though, the marks
of their presence could still be seen in a few hotels
and shops; the line of souvenir shops on the Corso
Umberto was broken now and then by a fairly elegant antique store or the sort of jewelry store in
which purchases are made at a desk rather than a

counter, in the manner of negotiating a corporate merger.

The writers' colony had dissolved over the years, leaving as traces a plaque here and there and an occasional art show and some Taormina people's memories of having met Thomas Mann or having had Truman Capote over for dinner. The local people who talked of Taormina's being spoiled were no longer talking about natives losing their own nice ways but about the chic and exotic going elsewhere.

"It used to be much more sophisticated," a man working at one of the hotels told me. "Now the middle classes are traveling more."

I nodded in sympathy. "I was saying as much to the *principessa* today," I said, "as she was selecting her *gelati*."

# 3

## Hanging Around
## in Uzès

I SUPPOSE I COULD SAY that we decided to take a house in the South of France for a month because it would give Abigail an opportunity to improve her French, but that would be like a newly rich business-man saying that he decided to buy a brand-new Cadillac El Dorado because a heavy car sticks to the road: it's true, but it's not the whole story.

Everyone in the family had some pleasant extra-educational daydreams of what life in the South of France might be like. In the one I most often clicked on in the months preceding our trip, I am sitting in an outdoor café on the town square sipping a drink, having somehow found some alcoholic beverage in a French café that does not taste like cough medicine. I am staring down at my drink in the significant way French intellectuals stare down at their drinks in cafés — either because they have just thought of something profoundly ironic or because they are wondering why they drink things that taste like cough medicine. Meanwhile, Abigail, then a tenth-grader with a couple of years of French under her belt, is scampering around the shops of the town to gather ingredients for the afternoon *pique-nique* — a French word I taught her myself, nearly exhausting my vocabulary in the process, on the theory that there are some things one cannot learn in school.

Sarah is with her, absorbing enough of that musical shopkeeper French (*Bonjour, madame; Merci, madame; Au revoir, madame*) to become the outstanding beginning French student in the next fall's seventh grade. Alice — who has just paid a visit to the local museum and made dinner reservations at a nearby two-star restaurant that happens to specialize in fish soup and done some window shopping (in my daydream, the only expensive women's clothing store in town happens to have an annual vacation closing that coincides precisely with the dates of our visit) and picked up some fresh *chèvre* from a wandering goat farmer — is about to join me at the café and to assure me that we are going to have the finest *pique-nique* in the history of the Republic, heavy on the *saucisson*. I, having at last thought of something profoundly ironic (perhaps the dates of the annual closing of the clothing store), lift my head and say, *"Quelle ironie!"* The other drinkers look up, nod, and draw up their lower lips in that French gesture of acknowledgment ("Well, the foreign-looking fellow is an intellectual after all"). Then we all go back to staring down at our drinks.

Until the trip was announced — we had found a house in a town called Uzès, about twenty miles from Avignon — Abigail and Sarah must have been pretty much resigned to seeing France only in daydreams. They had heard us say any number of times that children are ready to take a trip to France about the time they are ready to eat mushrooms. It was an opinion formed over the years by observing children who were being subjected to the Grand Tour of Europe — children who sat in formal hotel dining rooms doodling on the tablecloth with their butter knives, looking as if they were wondering whether there was any reason to hold out hope that they might be spared the second of tomorrow's scheduled cathedrals by a sudden downpour or perhaps a nuclear attack. We had not changed our view that staggering from hotel to sight to hotel to sight with the girls would be painful folly, but it had occurred to us that simply renting a house in a small town might be a sensible alternative — a way to be with the girls in France even before they were of an age to go through the Mushroom Passage.

By the time the plane landed in France, I was considering some arguments on the other side. During the flight across the Atlantic, the vision of the outdoor café had faded away, and in its place was a vision of me trying to deal with a particularly obdurate French plumber. The plumber is speaking very rapidly in French I don't understand. Abigail is consulting two different French-English dictionaries, and I am thumbing desperately through a phrase book that goes into great detail about how to send a cable from the post office but does not trouble to include the French for "stopped up."

Aside from the language barrier, my experiences in France had, to put it as politely as possible, not persuaded me that the French have a particularly strong tradition of friendliness and helpfulness toward visitors — even visitors with serious plumbing problems. So far, no scholar of Franco-American relations has attempted to refute the theory I once offered that some of the problems American visitors have with the French can be traced to the Hollywood movies of Maurice Chevalier. According to the theory, meeting a surly bureaucrat or a rude taxi driver is bound to be particularly disappointing if you've arrived with the expectation that every Frenchman you encounter will be a charming, debonair old gent who at any moment might start singing, "Sank Evan for leetle gerls."

Also, I realized almost immediately upon our arrival — it was at dinner on the terrace of a lovely country hotel we were spending the night in before driving on to our house — that my daydreams about life in France might have included the occasional two-star restaurant without including any information about what the girls were supposed to eat there. Quickly I fast-forwarded through the daydreams, searching for eating scenes. I found a scene of Abigail and Sarah going in the morning to the local bakery for croissants and *pains au chocolat*. There was a scene showing all of us gathered around a dinner table in the garden of our house to eat whatever we had collected at the stalls of the local market. But I couldn't find a scene that included Sarah, then a figure of some repute among fussy eaters, sitting in a grand restaurant.

As I snapped back into real time, I happened to glance at Sarah across the table. She seemed to be waiting in quiet trepidation, as if she expected at any moment to be required to consume a live asparagus. The expression on her face was the sort of expression associated with someone who might answer a question about whether he was enjoying his meal by saying, "Well, yes, warden, under the circumstances I am, and I do appreciate the effort you folks have made to make this meal special." Could it be, I wondered, that in an attempt at family togetherness we were about to turn our own daughter into a tablecloth doodler?

It had also occurred to me by then that American parents might be risking a serious guilt attack by bringing their children to Europe — at the cost of at least the extras on a brand-new Cadillac El Dorado — without injecting them with a full dose of what used to be called "cultural enrichment." I had seen the danger on the drive over, when we stopped for lunch at a village that happened to have a rather distinguished little church in it. After lunch we strolled into the church and gave the girls what I believe French intellectuals call "the Romanesque-Gothic rap." We spent a pleasant few minutes in the church, but after we emerged I happened to notice in the Michelin green guide that the time allotted for a viewing of the church interior was forty-five minutes. Forty-five minutes! We had just arrived, and we were already way behind.

I had figured that just living in a French town — getting the croissants every morning, searching out a parent who had absent-mindedly lingered in the café past dinnertime, maybe even dealing with an obdurate plumber — might qualify as culturally enriching, but I wasn't sure it measured up to the standards expected from the sort of American parents who wouldn't even bother with a village church as they ticked off the Big Sights. I envisioned a scene at JFK one month in the future as we presented ourselves to the immigration officer:

"You must have loved the Tower of London, little lady," the officer says to Sarah in a disarmingly friendly tone.

"We didn't actually go there," Sarah says.

"Well," he says, turning to Abigail with that same friendly air, "the Colosseum in Rome must have been pretty exciting."

"We were mainly just in this one town," Abigail says. Then, sensing trouble, she adds, "It was a very nice town."

The immigration officer turns to me, his voice coldly polite. "I'm afraid I'll have to hold on to this passport of yours for a while, sir," he says. "Just routine."

Uzès was indeed a very nice town — a market center of about seven thousand people in French farmland bearing an uncanny resemblance to a wine label. Best known as the site of the first duchy established in France, it still has a ducal palace with a multicolored roof that I rather admired even after I read in some Tweediesque guidebook that it was a "nineteenth-century error." Apparently, a ducal palace is not the sort of attraction that can deflect an overwhelming number of tourists who are bent on seeing the Palace of the Popes in Avignon and the Palace of the Grimaldis in Monte Carlo on the same day, so Uzès is a relatively peaceful place. In the still of the early evening, a visitor could have a drink in one of the cafés on the Place des Herbes, a vast and beautiful plaza right in the middle of town, and muse (at least in my case) on how his trepidations about taking a house in France were unfounded.

Our lack of fluency in French turned out not to be a problem: among four people, someone is bound to come up with the right word or gesture, and great command of the language is not required in order to point to a display of fluffy croissants and say, "Fourteen, please." After a couple of meals in good restaurants, we realized that even what seems to be the stuffiest French restaurant will always arrange to split a set meal between two children or to do up a simple piece of sole or even to produce, with some flourish, a ham sandwich. Sarah relaxed, as if there had been a last-minute reprieve from the governor.

Abigail and Sarah were, in fact, able to walk to the bakery every morning for croissants, since it was only three or four doors down the street. Our house was small and simple — a restored mid-nineteenth-century row house on an otherwise ungentrified block just off the main street of Uzès — but it turned out to be splendid. It had thick stone walls and a first-rate kitchen and precisely the garden I had imagined our having supper in every evening — a private little place, with a table underneath an arbor. The plumbing held up admirably — something I'll remember next time I get in one of those geopolitical discussions about whether the French can be depended on.

My concerns about providing sufficient cultural enrichment turned out to be the easiest to deal with. Every afternoon I simply informed the girls of what they were missing that day by not being on the Grand Tour. "It's Rome today, *jeunes filles*," I would say as we sat next to one of our favorite swimming spots on the Gard River, just after a splendid picnic (heavy on the *saucisson*). "The Trevi Fountain! There it is — excellent fountain, excellent. The Spanish Steps. Watch it there, mister, don't shove. Plenty of room for everybody, at least there would be if you people didn't travel in regiments in those damn tour buses. Okay, girls, we'll want to take in the Colosseum while it's still there. On to the Vatican. Whoops! A lot of traffic around the Vatican. Awfully hot in Rome this time of year, particularly with the traffic. I don't think I've ever been so hot."

"In that case, Daddy," one of the girls would say, "maybe we should just get in the water."

By switching swimming holes one day, I was able to present a real rather than imaginary sight of Grand Tour proportions. "Look above you," I said, pointing up at the Pont du Gard. "That's the best-preserved Roman aqueduct in the world, seen from the authentic angle of a Roman slave who fell off it during construction."

I don't mean to imply that we ignored the sights in our vicinity that were not observable from a backstroke. On a sunny morning we might take a drive that combined an outdoor lunch and a stroll with a visit to, say, the Palace of the Popes in Avignon or a castle we had been admiring in Tarascon or the Roman arena in Nîmes or the medieval village of Les Baux. "Life is not all *pain au chocolat,* ladies," I would announce at breakfast. "We are about to endeavor to stuff a little culture down you."

I also don't mean to imply that my notion about the cultural enrichment of simply living in a French town proved to be one of those brilliantly simple theories that work without qualification. There is a fuzzy line, it turns out, between an experience that seems interesting in the French version ("Isn't it interesting to see a French supermarket?" I would say, ecstatic at the sight of bins full of ninety-cent wine) and experiences that may best be described in the remark "You didn't come all the way to France to play miniature golf." Where the line is drawn obviously depends on who does the drawing — a fact brought home to me one day as we were walking past a line of gumball machines and Sarah said, "Wouldn't it be interesting to try French bubble gum!"

"Uh-oh," I thought. "She's broken the code."

Instead of miniature golf, we played what the French call *babyfoot*, a two-franc soccer game in which you drive the ball toward your opponent's goal by flipping miniature players attached to rods. Our approach to being in France carried with it, I suppose, a bias toward doing things rather than seeing things, toward being in places where something was happening rather than being in places where something once happened. We liked the splendidly preserved Roman arena of Nîmes when we strolled through it almost alone one quiet Sunday. We liked it even better when we sat in it a few days later to watch a traveling European circus that had an American theme — including a troupe of knockabout acrobats who were dressed in double-breasted blue suits and were constantly shooting blanks at each other from snub-nosed revolvers and were called Le Chicago. The acrobatic act may have been the inspiration for the device I found myself using to strike terror into the heart of any shopkeeper or minor official who displeased me: I'd make a pistol out of my thumb and forefinger, cock my thumb, say "She-ca-go," and walk away.

Our approach meant spending a lot of time at the morning market, checking to see which farmer had brought in the best tomatoes. It involved going to any local event that sounded at all intriguing — including a Saturday-night jollity called *taureaux piscine*, which struck me as impossible to describe to an immigration officer who was expecting youthful impressions of Big Ben and Versailles and the Colosseum. ("Yes, that's what I'm saying — sort of a plastic swimming pool right in the middle of the bullring . . .") It meant taking a lot of evening strolls that didn't have any particular destination, and lingering in the garden over suppers that reflected more shopping than cooking — salad and cheese from the market, and the local wine, and, for the girls, those French versions of pizza that in the South of France seem to be turned out in every bakery and even a few butcher shops. In other words, we hung around.

When we visited nearby towns, I realized that hanging around is not an activity covered well by guidebooks. I don't mean that I'm not interested in the sort of information offered by guidebooks that emphasize history and architecture. The scenes of van Gogh's paintings were somehow more interesting to me after I read that when van Gogh cut off his ear, he knocked on the door of a woman he knew in Arles, presented her with the ear, said, "Guard this precious item," and disappeared into the night. I'm also interested, though, in a lot of information guidebooks don't seem to have — when the town has its market day and whether there's a good annual celebration and where you can find the best street for strolling. I'd like to know which of the town cafés caters to soccer fans and which to *boules* players and which to the cycling crowd and which to intellectuals who stare significantly down at their cough medicine. The guidebook we could have used for our day trips from Uzès would be called *The Hanging Around Guide to France*, first in a series.

In Uzès itself, of course, we eventually found the best strolling streets and the best *babyfoot* game — in the soccer fans' café, where middle-aged men sat quietly enjoying a drink or playing cards and the walls were decorated with league schedules and group pictures of the Uzès squad. Once found, our favorite places became part of a routine. One of the essential differences between the Grand Tour and the Hanging Around approaches to being in Europe is the attitude toward repeat visits. On the Grand Tour, you go once. You don't go back to Notre Dame once you've seen Notre Dame. Once you've seen Notre Dame, you go to the Louvre. In Hanging Around, repetition is part of the pleasure. If you find a nice local museum — like the Museon Arlaten in Arles — you go back now and then. If you find a *pommes frites* stand that reminds you why French fries were named after the French, you make it a regular stop on the evening stroll. In a few days it becomes natural to say, "I'll meet you at our *pommes frites* stand."

There came a time in Uzès when it became natural to think of a lot of things around town as our things. Saturday is the market day in the Place des Herbes, and we had been there enough Saturdays to decide which was our *saucisson* stand and which was our baker. Thanks to some local kids Abigail and Sarah met at the river, we had discovered what would obviously be our swimming hole. Our evening routine had become pretty well set. We stopped at our *pommes frites* stand, got two orders to go, and then adjourned to a place on the Place des Herbes that made fruit drinks in a blender — our fruit-drink place. We would have supper in the garden and then, maybe, a game of *babyfoot* at the soccer bar. Over the *babyfoot* game one evening toward the end of our stay — Alice had remained at the house to finish a book, and I was playing against Abigail and Sarah — it occurred to me that things had worked out more like the daydreams of the spring than the horrifying visions on the day of our arrival. Abigail had been chattering away in French to the kids at the river and had taken charge of making restaurant reservations over the telephone in French. Sarah knew every word in French that could be used to describe a flavor of ice cream, as she demonstrated later in the summer when, during a North American picnic lunch at which raspberry Kool-Aid was being served, she said, "Please pass the *framboise*." In the subtle negotiations that occur when time is up for grabs rather than strictly allotted, Alice had got her share of scenic drives and the girls had got their share of swims and I had got my share of fish soup.

The other way to look at it, I realized at almost the same moment, was that we had brought our children to France to hang out in bars and live on French fries and take-out pizza. At that moment Sarah drilled one past my goalie, giving her and Abigail the game. Hanging out in bars and beating their elders at two-franc soccer games! I looked up from the goal. "*Quelle ironie!*" I said.

# 4

## Damp in
## the Afternoon

WHEN I BEGAN TRYING to describe *taureaux pi-scine* to people in America, I was struck by how many of them had precisely the same response: "You have to be kidding!" I'll admit that I might have been tempted to use that phrase myself when *taureaux piscine* first came to my attention, except that my French wouldn't have been up to it. My French isn't up to a lot, although I know a number of nouns. I probably just shook my head in amazement, or did my imperfect imitation of that look Frenchmen in cafés use to indicate without a word that what has just been said may well be true for the simple reason that so many other silly things are.

This happened one Saturday, market day, in Uzès. I was sitting with Alice and Abigail and Sarah in an outdoor café we favored on Saturdays for its proximity to our market-day *pommes frites* specialist, a thorough craftsman who would not consider offering a customer a sackful of French fries until he had fried them at least twice. On a tree next to our table, a handwritten sign announced an event that would take place in the local arena at nine that night: TAUREAUX PISCINE. I do not have to be kidding.

I had been under the impression that both *taureaux* and *piscine* were among my nouns, but I couldn't think of any way to translate them except as "bulls" and "swimming pool." The next time our table was visited by the café's proprietress, a woman who had already demonstrated her good nature by a tolerant view of carried-in *pommes frites*, I tried to get some more information. *"Taureaux comme taureaux?"* I asked, using my fingers as horns to do a passable imitation of a fighting bull. (I know several conjunctions; it's verbs I don't do.)

*"Oui, monsieur,"* she said.

*"Piscine comme piscine?"* I went on, demonstrating with an Esther Williams breaststroke that I happen to do almost flawlessly as long as I'm out of the water.

*"Oui, monsieur."*

She bustled off to see to her other customers, leaving me with a lot of questions unexpressed and, for me in French, unexpressible. I knew that the South of France, particularly the area toward the mouth of the Rhône, had its own tradition of Provençal tauromachy. I suppose you could say that the South of France, particularly the Côte d'Azur, has its own tradition of swimming pools. But how would the two go together? Why would the two go together?

The answers were not immediately forthcoming. As it happened, we were unable to attend the *taureaux piscine* being held in the arena that evening. We did have a couple of English-speaking acquaintances who had lived in Uzès for some time, but they had never heard of *taureaux piscine*. I made a careful survey of wall posters in Uzès and in any other town we happened to drive through that next week. No *taureaux piscine*. I began to think that I had missed the opportunity to see a unique coupling of bulls and swimming pool. It occurred to me that I might be left with only that astounding name — *taureaux piscine*. Aside from the energy it produced with its jarring juxtaposition, it had struck me from the start as a name of great euphony. It was clearly at its best when used as something like a war cry, with all four syllables plainly and loudly enunciated — "TAU-REAUX-PI-SCINE!" In fact, as we drove through the countryside around Uzès, I occasionally found myself shouting "TAU-REAUX-PI-SCINE" out the car window into the wind, as if to announce to the residents of the next village what my quest was. The next Saturday was our last Saturday in Uzès. We went to the same café. I saw the same sign on the same tree: TAUREAUX PISCINE.

We arrived at the arena late. By chance, we had guests that weekend, and some of them were reluctant to rush through dinner, even though I kept telling them that, for all we knew about *taureaux piscine*, the best part might be right at the beginning. The arena looked like the bullfight arena of a Spanish provincial town except, of course, that in the middle of the ring there was a swimming pool — a rather small swimming pool, with only a couple of feet of water in it, but still a swimming pool. From the stands it looked like one of those plastic swimming pools that people in the suburbs buy at the discount store and stick out in the back yard for the smaller kids to splash around in. There were a few dozen teenage boys in the ring. There was also a bull — a small bull, with blunts on the points of his horns, but still a bull. In other words, the bull in *taureaux piscine* was a bull, and the swimming pool was a swimming pool. Upon my oath.

Within a few minutes it was clear that *taureaux piscine* has an extraordinary aspect that I had not anticipated during the week I'd spent simply amazed at its existence and enamored of its name. It is the

only sport I have ever encountered that has only one
rule: If you and the bull are in the pool at the same
time, you win. If you do it again, you win again; a
limitation of the rule would require a second rule.

The boys in the ring that night seemed to be having trouble winning. An announcer talked constantly
over a public address system — exhorting the boys,
taunting the boys, praising the bull, increasing the
number of francs that would go to anybody who
managed to share the pool with the bull. The boys,
most of whom were dressed in blue jeans and
T-shirts, spent a lot of time jumping up and down
to attract the bull's attention and a lot of time running from the bull once they had it — usually end-
ing the run by leaping over the inner fence that
separates the ring from the stands in a bullfight
arena. Occasionally, two or three of them would
simply stand in the pool waiting for the bull to join
them — like those towering but ungainly centers in
the earlier days of basketball who planted themselves under the basket — and would have second
thoughts about the strategy once the bull actually
approached.

Suddenly, one boy, realizing that he had attracted
the bull's attention from just the right angle, started
his run toward the *piscine* simultaneously with the
bull's charge and dived in head first just as the bull
rumbled through the water. I thought it was a bril-

liant, daring move — something I might have been tempted to describe, if I had been a fan of longer duration, as "what *taureaux piscine* is all about."

I have to say that it was not enough to make *taureaux piscine* enthusiasts out of my companions. Alice and Abigail agreed that *taureaux piscine* was at least boring and maybe cruel. Sarah gazed upon the goings-on as she might have gazed upon a mixed-vegetable plate. One of our guests said that *taureaux piscine* was a mess. Somebody in our party, I am obligated to report, said to me, "You have to be kidding!" even after he had seen *taureaux piscine* with his own eyes.

I liked it. Of course, as someone who had spent a week in a state of excitement over the very existence of *taureaux piscine*, I might have been expected to have a certain proprietary feeling about it. That did not blind me to its faults. "I'll admit it lacks finesse," I said after the head-first hero had shaken himself off, collected forty francs from the announcer, and rejoined his fellows. Still, how could anybody fail to be engaged by it? It provoked so many questions. How, for instance, had *taureaux piscine* come about? It was as if a game had been invented by the wild man in the old-fashioned Hollywood story conference — the one who's there to come up with something like "I've got it! Her long-lost father is the King of England," so that someone else is jogged into saying, "Well, not the King of England, but some sort of English aristocrat might not be a bad idea." The wild man says, "Here it is — a bull and a swimming pool," and for some reason nobody says, "Not a swimming pool, Harry, but we could have a nice little obstacle course or something like that." Why had Americans spent so much time and energy analyzing the Spanish bullfight while completely ignoring *taureaux piscine*? I intended to take care of that oversight the following summer. During the winter, while driving along turnpikes, I occasionally opened the window and shouted, "TAU-REAUX-PI-SCINE," just to keep my hand in.

It's not as if you could just call up the United Taureaux Piscine League and ask for the summer schedule. We were back in France the next June, but I couldn't seem to find any *taureaux piscine*. We were staying in a town just east of the Rhône, still in the part of Provence where any good-sized village is likely to have both a bullfight arena and a café that serves as headquarters for the local *club taurin*. There was no shortage of posters with pictures of bulls on them. It was already high season for the Provençal version of bullfighting, which is often called La Course Camarguaise — after the Camargue, a vast salt marsh in the Rhône delta, where most of the bulls are raised. A French bullfight isn't exactly a fight. There are no swords or capes or elaborate costumes. In the variety that has become an organized professional sport, the bull has a sort of rosette, called a *cocarde*, attached to his horns; the participants — men who are dressed in white pants and white T-shirts and white sneakers — run in a long arc that passes in front of the bull, try to snatch off the *cocarde* with what amounts to a comb, and then try to get themselves over the barrier before the bull can demonstrate his displeasure.

The participants, called *rasateurs*, are competing against one another rather than against the bull; they amass point totals that are listed regularly in the newspapers, like the winnings of professional golfers. The leading *rasateurs* become famous in Provence, as do the leading bulls. *Rasateurs* are not in the least embarrassed by having to leap over the barrier all the time. A Spanish matador who ran out of the ring, of course, might as well just keep going, but for a French *rasateur*, carrying only a four-inch comb by way of protection, a *coup de barrière* is the logical exit. In the magazines devoted to La Course Camarguaise — I read a number of them, looking for notices of *taureaux piscine* — nearly every picture seems to be of a *rasateur* leaping over the barrier toward the stands, followed at a distance of an inch or two by an angry bull. It would be gratifying,

I suppose, to report that the French version of tauromachy — sporting, nonlethal, good-humored, relatively unpretentious — is more exciting than the
Spanish *corrida*. But I found that a little of it goes a
long way. For my money, I thought as I watched
some celebrated *rasateurs* go through their paces
one afternoon, the performance could be improved
greatly by the simple addition of a swimming pool.

In my search for *taureaux piscine*, I found that
the French, not being locked into bullfighting as a
ritual, had developed all sorts of variations on the
theme of La Course Camarguaise. Particularly during a festival, a Provençal town is likely to complement the performance of the *rasateurs* with less formal events, which are designed to include anyone
who feels like having a go. In the simplest form, a
small bull or cow is let out into the ring, and
the local boys swerve in front of it on their way to
the barrier — trying to pick off a *cocarde*, or, in the
more common version, simply trying to show how
close they can get. A number of games take off from
there. Lydie Marshall, a French-born friend of ours
who had volunteered to act as a provider of verbs for
my quest while she was visiting us in Provence,
tracked down a friend of hers who had participated
in a game called *taureaux pastèque*, or *taureaux*
watermelon. It's one of those games that sound simple but turn out to be complicated. Every contestant

is given a piece of watermelon to eat, and the one who finishes first wins. That's the simple part. The complicating factors are that the watermelon can be eaten only while the contestant is seated on a bench, the bench is in the bullring, and so is a bull. One of the games I heard about sounded almost as ingeniously simple as *taureaux piscine*. It's called *taureaux football*. Two teams engage in a game of soccer. The only difference from conventional soccer is that there's a bull in the ring.

I had a certain amount of curiosity about *taureaux football*. It was obviously a game that could include some subtle strategic wrinkles. For instance, would the best strategy be simply to play soccer, glancing over your shoulder regularly for the bull, or would the best strategy be to have one man stand behind the opposing goalie and try to attract the bull's attention?

I did not let my curiosity about *taureaux football* deflect me from the thrust of my research — *taureaux piscine*. Where was it? I got some guidance from a woman we fell into conversation with in a town called Eyragues while watching an *abrivado* — an entertainment in which a bull is run up and down a street within a phalanx of Camarguaise horsemen while the brave lads of the town try to pry him from his blockers, sometimes by the tail. She said that *taureaux piscine* was much more common toward July, when the evenings could be counted on to be warm. Of course! I should have realized that a sport requiring its successful participants to run around in soaking-wet clothing had to be played in warm weather. It was clear that I could not yet be described as a true student of the game.

I had never thought of looking for *taureaux piscine* at the Nîmes Feria. Nîmes, along with a few other places in Provence, regularly stages absolutely traditional Spanish *corridas* — its Roman arena is even better suited to that than to the acrobatics of Le Chicago — and the Feria is a festive week of Spanish bullfighting that can inspire some citizens to talk about how much the people of Nîmes have in common with the people of Seville. The Feria always presents leading Spanish matadors. The bulls are from illustrious Andalusian bull ranches. The press coverage is marked by the sort of purple *corrida* prose I have treasured ever since I read, many years ago in Seville, that a matador named Diego Puerta had in his fight the previous day "written brilliant pages in the book of valor." During the Feria, we read in the local newspaper that "the presentation of Curro Caro was a sonnet of artistic success" and that "in the space of an instant, no more, but an instant that seemed an eternity, with the fourth bull

Emilio Muñoz created a masterpiecé of purity." I couldn't see where *taureaux piscine* would fit in with talk like that. Then, toward the end of the Feria, I happened to glance through the schedule of events and saw that there was a *taureaux piscine* that very evening at eight o'clock. We headed for Nîmes.

The *taureaux piscine* was not being held in the Roman arena. It was in a small arena that belonged to the Nîmes bullfighting school. During the Feria, the bullfight-school arena was the last stop along a sort of midway of food booths and carnival rides and a bandstand that featured, the evening we were there, Alain May et les Mod Beats. Lydie quickly found the man in charge — Lucien Moulin, who worked for the city of Alès, twenty-five miles or so north of Nîmes, and staged *taureaux piscines* on the side. Moulin said that for the Feria he had arranged and announced five *taureaux piscines* a day, each with six bulls — a pace so grueling that he had abandoned his normal practice of introducing each bull with his own trumpet fanfare and settled for a taped rendition over the public address system. The *taureaux piscine* we saw him put on was squarely in the tradition of what I remembered from Uzès, although with a closer look I realized that the swimming pool was made not of plastic but of hay bales and a canvas tarp. Moulin spoke constantly over the public address system, providing play-by-play and offers of great rewards from various sponsors and

taunts for the brave young men and jokes that tended
to dwell on mothers-in-law or on the potential conse-
quences of being followed very closely by a bull. Occasionally, a triumphant young man would stand
before Moulin, dripping wet, to be tossed fifty or
sixty francs in coins. I thought that one tall boy
wearing blue jeans but no shirt might be said to
have written brilliant pages in the book of valor
if he hadn't slipped a bit in the mud that forms from
the splashing just outside the pool. A boy wearing a
T-shirt that said ÉCOUTEZ RADIO 102 made a leap toward the pool that I would consider at least a rhym-
ing couplet of artistic success.

After the last bull had left the ring, we had a chat
with Moulin. I was hoping to learn something of how
*taureaux piscine* had developed — from a chance
puddle at a Camarguaise bull ranch, maybe, or
through some old Provençal connection between
bulls and rivers that I hadn't yet put together. When
I asked if special bulls were required, Moulin said he
always got his bulls from Jean-Marie Bilhau, whose
father, Émile, had invented *taureaux piscine*.

"Did he say 'invented *taureaux piscine*'?" I asked
Lydie.

"That's what he said," Lydie replied.

Invented *taureaux piscine*! There was an inventor
of *taureaux piscine*! I asked Moulin if Émile Bilhau
was still alive. Moulin said that the elder Bilhau was
up in years but still quite active. I could presumably

drive down to his place, near Saint-Gilles, and have a chat with him. I felt like a baseball nut who had just been told that it wouldn't be any problem to have a beer with Abner Doubleday.

Saint-Gilles turned out to be a town whose signs identified it as Gateway to the Camargue and City of Roman Art. I found Émile Bilhau a few miles outside of town in a place called Mas d'Estagel — a place that began as a medieval monastery, was converted into a hotel, and was then converted by Bilhau and his wife into a kind of rural catering hall for parties and special events. The buildings were surrounded by fields and vineyards. Next to a sort of picnic ground for outdoor parties was a roughly made bullring. Émile Bilhau turned out to be a small, straightforward country man who looked something like a Camarguaise version of Barry Fitzgerald. He said he had been interested in horses and bulls all his life; as a young man, he told us, he became the only rider in France who could leap from a horse onto the back of a bull, a trick he picked up from watching a visiting American rodeo. He acknowledged that he was indeed the inventor of *taureaux piscine*. While I was taking that in, he added that he had invented *taureaux football* as well. He had nothing to do with *taureaux* watermelon.

It all came about, he said, while he was managing the arenas at Saint-Gilles and Les Saintes-Maries-de-la-Mer, a Camarguaise seaside resort that is particularly well known for taurine events. He had decided that the *courses de nuit* — the amateur events held in the evening during the festivals — were boring. A lot of young men just ran around with bulls; nobody in the stands knew exactly what was going on. The solution he came up with, in 1957 or 1958, was *taureaux piscine*. In other words, *taureaux piscine* had come about for the same reason that, say, Ladies' Day in baseball had come about — as a way to build the gate. I liked that. It did not lack finesse.

Bilhau had decided that any of the games could be improved by an announcer. The announcer, he said, was the key to *taureaux piscine* — the person who involved both the participants and the audience. Bilhau, of course, had been the first announcer. One of his trademarks, he told us, was picking out young men in the ring and giving them heroic names — Napoleon, maybe, or Charlemagne. He said he still announced occasionally, but ordinarily he contented himself with renting out bulls to other *taureaux piscine* promoters. He could also furnish the hay bales and the specially designed tarp for the pool — a contraption that, it almost goes without saying, he invented.

But how, I asked, had he come up with his greatest stroke of invention, the combination of bulls and swimming pool?

"I wanted to find the comical point of view," Bilhau said. "What is there that's comical? There's water. There's a custard pie."

If Abner Doubleday could have expressed himself that succinctly, I suspect, baseball would not be so difficult for foreigners to understand. I was definitely in the presence of the inventor, a man who could have tossed off *taureaux* custard pie if he had been in the mood. I decided that Saint-Gilles should add to its sobriquets. It was not simply Gateway to the Camargue and City of Roman Art. It was also Birthplace of Taureaux Piscine.

I met Jean-Marie Bilhau, Émile's son, the next Sunday. A local *club taurin* was holding a *ferrade* at Mas d'Estagel, and the elder Bilhau had invited our whole family to attend. A *ferrade* is a sort of informal rodeo and picnic; in the principal event, calves run across a large field toward a branding fire, and horsemen try to push them over with long poles that look like jousters' lances. Jean-Marie told me that *taureaux piscine* had been a great hit in Barcelona and that he had plans to take it to Germany and Italy. He asked me how I thought it would go over in America. It was not a question I had considered. "You have bulls there, right?" Jean-Marie asked.

I told him our bulls were less the sort that charged young men than the sort whose back you jumped onto from a horse. He said that bringing along his own bulls would be no problem; the Spanish had invented a sort of box to carry bulls on airplanes. I suppose the second generation is always more technologically oriented.

"America is ready for *taureaux piscine*," he said.

"You may be right," I said.

I was just being polite. But the more I thought about it, as we drove through the vineyards away from Mas d'Estagel, the more clearly I could see *taureaux piscine* in America — the analytical stories in the sports section, the opening night at some place like Madison Square Garden, the interview on local TV with some soaking-wet hero from the Bronx. I opened the window of the car. I shouted into the wind, "TAU-REAUX-PI-SCINE!"

# 5

# For Queen and Fritter

"DID YOU SAY 'eat in the hotel'?" I asked. There was always a chance that I had misunderstood, although not much of one. Alice, who under ordinary circumstances wouldn't think of eating dinner in a hotel dining room, has an unshakable belief that the hotel is the only place to have your first meal after a day spent traveling to a foreign country. I pointed out that the journey we had just made, from New York to Barbados, was approximately the same distance as a trip from New York to Utah, and that what we were about to do was therefore the equivalent of having dinner in the dining room of the Salt Lake City Ramada Inn.

I also pointed out that Barbados was so strongly influenced by the English, who ruled it for three

centuries, that it is sometimes known as Little England — meaning that dinner at a Barbados hotel
was likely to consist of any number of formally
served courses, each of which could make one yearn
for the Ramada Inn's soup 'n' sandwich special. I
didn't expect Alice's plans to be affected in the least
by those arguments. She has always observed the
custom of eating in the hotel on the night of our arrival as if she were observing a sacrament central to
some religion — a religion that has never been identified but must have something to do with mortifica-
tion of the flesh.

It happened to be the hotel's night for a buffet. As
we approached the food that had been laid out on
the buffet tables, it occurred to me that if the sons of
lieutenant colonels in the Coldstream Guards had
bar mitzvahs, this is what the reception spread would
look like. The display reflected the extraordinary
care the English have always taken with the appearance of special-occasion victuals; their interest in
food tends to peak just before the eating. There were
slices of cold salmon that had been cut into fish
shapes and given eyes made out of a material that
could be eaten, although, like the salmon itself, not
tasted. There were several ice sculptures, confirming
my impression that the number of English sculptors
on the international art scene is always limited by
the fact that so many of them are kept busy fashion-

ing sea bass out of ice. There was roast beef and York-shire pudding and creamed cauliflower and Brussels sprouts. I stopped in front of the Brussels sprouts and stared at them for a while. "The English have a lot to answer for," I said to Alice. It's amazing to me that with all the issues that brought colonial people out in the street during the long hegemony of the British Empire, nobody ever rebelled against Brussels sprouts. Or maybe somebody did. Maybe in those old newsreel clips that show hordes of chanting demonstrators rushing through the streets in the days before independence, what they are actually chanting is not "British go home!" or "Down with the Raj!" but "No more Brussels sprouts!"

In the early eighties, when I revealed publicly that I often daydream of what life in the Caribbean would be like if there were an Italian West Indies — the I.W.I. vacation spot I envision, a lush volcanic island whose steep hills are green with garlic plants, is called Santo Prosciutto — I just about convinced myself that the British might respond by giving Italy, say, Tortola. ("No, please, we want you to have it. The soil's no good for growing overcooked cabbage anyhow.") When it comes to eating in the Carib-bean, I seem to be afflicted with an optimism that flies in the face of personal experience. Somehow, I always arrive for my first visit on a Caribbean is-land confident that once I've put the mandatory hotel meal behind me I am going to find something decent to eat.

When we arrived in Barbados, Alice reminded me that even my most frenzied efforts in the Caribbean tend not to be fruitful. She said that without even knowing that once — when, through some odd circumstances, she and I and Abigail and Sarah had been given the opportunity to spend a week together on St. Thomas, in the American Virgin Islands — I had made some secret forays based on the admittedly faint possibility that some Danish chef, known equally for his stubbornness and his shellfish dishes, had remained after Denmark sold the islands to the United States in 1917 and was still plying his trade in a restaurant that was virtually unknown on the island (because he refused to print his menu in English) but attracted knowing gourmets from Copenhagen.

"Don't forget the bullfoot soup," she said, referring to a native dish on St. Thomas whose name, I'm afraid, described it with unfortunate precision.

"Well, I'm sure at least that it was authentic," I said. "It tasted pretty much the way you'd imagine something called bullfoot soup tasting. And there was, of course, the undeniable presence of the foot . . ."

Alice's point, of course, was that this desperate search negates the reason for coming to the Caribbean in the first place — relaxation. I admitted long ago that I have been among those men the cartoonists show sitting on a Caribbean beach listening to their wives telling them to relax. The difference is that the others are worried about the business they were supposed to have left behind — they are popping up from the sand every five minutes to try to get through to the office in order to offer one last thought on the Perkins account; they are shouting at the beachboy for working in a place that does not receive the *Wall Street Journal* on the days it's printed — and I am tending to the business at hand.

In Barbados, for instance, I had used the ride in from the airport to scan the horizon for land that was planted in something more immediately useful than sugar cane, and to question the driver closely about where he ate when he happened to find himself in Bridgetown, the capital, around lunchtime. I thought I had reason for optimism. Barbados, after all, is noted for its use of a local fish; the motto being promoted by its tourist office was "Land of the Flying Fish." I have been to Caribbean islands whose motto should be "Land of the Frozen Fillet." In New York, we had been told by someone who lived for many years in Barbados that Barbadians — or Bajans, as they are often called — have in recent years moved away from the traditions of Little England toward a more Caribbean culture of their own. I had read in a guidebook that even hotels had become more willing to put Bajan specialties like fishballs or pepperpot on their menus. One of the restaurant advertisements I saw while thumbing through the local paper during our first day on the beach was for a place that specialized in what was described as "Nu Bajan Cuisine."

"This is a good sign," I said, showing the advertisement to Alice. "If there's a new Bajan cuisine, it stands to reason that there must be an old Bajan cuisine." I couldn't imagine, for instance, St. Thomas having a new Thomian cuisine — unless it consisted of a large white plate upon which was a perfect strawberry, some sliced kiwi, and, in the center, a single bullfoot. I told Alice that I had high hopes. The taxi driver who brought us from the airport had given me a tip on a Bridgetown place where I might find Bajan specialties like peas-and-rice and cou-cou, a sort of pudding made out of cornmeal and okra. We had the name of a hotel on the Atlantic shore that specialized in a Bajan buffet. I had been told about a street in Bridgetown called Baxter's Road, where Bajans go late at night to eat and drink in small bars or to buy fried fish from women who cook over kettles of embers right on the street. I admitted to Alice that I was a bit worried about being able to stay up late enough to make it to Baxter's Road.

"Couldn't you just relax?" she said.

"It's hard," I said. "Brussels sprouts make me jumpy."

❦

"Well, this was educational," I said after we had finished the Bajan buffet at the Atlantic shore hotel. "Although I'm not sure that's the highest compliment I've ever given a meal." The Atlantic coast of Barbados is spectacular — a largely undeveloped stretch of beach with huge rock formations and a powerful surf. Just below the hotel, fishermen were bringing in their day's catch of flying fish. The buffet included a number of local specialties — spinach cakes, pumpkin fritters, peas-and-rice, pickled bananas — along with a few surprises, like chow mein. The educational aspect was that each dish had in front of it a neatly printed identification sign. Although the signs did not include the proper Latin name for, say, pickled bananas (*Ananum piclum*), it was a bit like wandering around a well-marked botanical garden with a plate in your hand.

By then I had found quite a bit to eat in Barbados that was not Brussels sprouts. I had eaten some first-rate fried dorado, a fish the Bajans refer to as dolphin. At the taxi driver's place in Bridgetown, I had been introduced to a flying-fish cutter, a cutter being a sandwich made on a high, squarish roll. At the Cheapside public market — a place that looked like my vision of a West African market, with women in print dresses sitting behind displays of odd-looking root vegetables or strolling down the long aisles between the stalls with baskets of breadfruit on their heads — I sampled a remarkable variety of spicy fishballs from tiny lunch stands with names like Nic's Snackette. I had eaten what I took to be fried squid in a dish listed on the menu of a little beach bar as "Scuttle à la Earlene (Chef's Delight)." I had eaten a noted Bajan dish called pudding and souse, which is made from a lot of little-used pig parts that it probably wouldn't hurt to waste. Still, I thought I had to go to Baxter's Road, which, I had been told, didn't start bustling until midnight. After a day in the sun, it's not easy to stay up until midnight, particularly when someone keeps telling you to relax.

Bajans love to stay up late. I suppose part of the entertainment on Baxter's Road is speculating on where the other celebrants were before they decided to start eating chicken at three in the morning. Judging from the local paper, a lot of them were dancing. On the Friday I decided to go to Baxter's Road, the paper carried a page or two of advertisements for dances available to anyone willing to pay an admission charge of five dollars Barbadian — about two-fifty American. Each ad showed a picture of the dance's organizer, who was identified not simply by name but by nickname and sometimes by place of work or automobile license-plate number — so that the invitation might come from "Mr. Keith Sandiford (known as Nobby)" or "Miss Yvette Yearwood (known as Sugary)" or "Mr. Sylvan Greenidge (known as Nat Cole)" or "Mr. Edgar McClean (better known as Sheriff), bus driver of Transport Board on Route 22A." Nobby and Nat Cole and Sugary and Sheriff and the rest were presumably still on the dance floor when I arrived at Baxter's Road, because I had decided that if I didn't start out by ten I might not start out at all.

Baxter's Road turned out to be a collection of small bars and restaurants and stores, most of them open only at night. The architecture was a rickety version of that diminutive Caribbean style that appears to be based on telling the builder to do everything in three-fifths scale. The establishments on Baxter's Road had names like Kool Hour Bar & Restaurant and Tip Top Restaurant & Bar and John's Night Cap. The light came mainly from the bars and restaurants, most of which were completely open to the street. The smell of smoke and spices drifted down from the top of the road, where a dozen or so women stood in the dark on the pavement, frying fish over wood fires and chanting for customers, as if practicing a forbidden religion in a country where the British colonial administration may have left the natives thoroughly grounded in English cooking

as a punishment for consistently winning cricket
matches against the people who taught them the
game. The total effect could make a visitor feel for a
moment that he had wandered onto a set for *Porgy
and Bess*.

I was there by myself, reconnoitering. If Baxter's
Road fulfilled my expectations, I was planning to
bring Alice back the next night. I made my headquarters in Enid's Bar, a place recommended to me
for its fried chicken. It amounted to a tiny room,
with a bar and three tables and a large sign that read
PLEASE DO NOT PUT YOUR FOOT ON THE CHAIR OR SIT
ON TABLE. A large, cheerful woman named Shirley
was presiding, opening the display case on the bar
now and then as someone walked in off the street
and asked for a flying-fish cutter or some cold chicken
necks or pudding and souse or a bottle of beer or a
type of coconut roll that is called, ominously, a lead
pipe.

The only other customer at the bar at that hour
was an American named Glenn, who had lived in
Barbados for ten years. He acted as a sort of interpreter, since Shirley's English was delivered in such
a thick Bajan accent that I sometimes didn't understand her. At one point in the evening, for instance,
I returned from taking a turn of the street and asked
Shirley if she knew what was in the sandwich that
seemed to be the specialty of a place named the Pink

Star — a huge loaf called a one-fifty, after its price. When she answered, I turned to Glenn and said, "Did she say, 'They boils up livers and gizzards and they put them in there'?"

Glenn nodded. "I'm afraid so," he said.

I decided that I was too full for a one-fifty. After all, I had already sampled some spectacular fried fish at the top of the road, and I had eaten a few chicken livers, and I had just asked Shirley if she would mind frying some chicken for me, even though Nobby and Nat Cole and the rest of the regular fried-chicken customers were still nowhere in sight. When she put the chicken in front of me, maybe twenty minutes later, she watched me eat a few bites and then asked what I thought.

"I think I'll be back here with my wife tomorrow night," I said.

Shirley had told me that even though there are few early-evening customers, the fish hawkers set up their operations around eight, and that she had been known to begin frying chicken soon after she opened the doors at nine. We were at Enid's the next night when it opened. Before that, we had stopped at the fish fryers for some fried dolphin, served in a paper bag. Alice acknowledged that it was about the finest piece of fried fish she had ever eaten. You could hear the appreciation in her voice when she turned to the woman who had sold it to us and said, "What are these spices?"

The woman laughed. "That's my little secret, dearie," she said.

The chicken at Enid's was splendid, pan-fried slowly in the spicy batter Bajans like. Alice downed it with dispatch — an impressive performance, considering that she had passed some of the frying time polishing off some warmed-up chicken gizzards as an appetizer. When she finished, she sat back satisfied, although resisting any temptation she might have had to put her foot on the chair in front of her. I also felt satisfied. The search had been worth the effort. I was, in fact, almost relaxed. Then I began to consider the possibility that I had not really looked hard enough on St. Thomas.

# 6

## Prix du Hamburger

"WELL, IT SMELLS exactly like McDonald's," Sarah said.

The rest of the company nodded and murmured assent. We were on the Champs-Élysées, at a restaurant called Freetime — a French-owned fast-food operation that offered Les Superhits, including a Hitburger and a Hitfrench (*"même préparation que le Hitburger, avec des herbes de Provence"*). Sarah was then eleven or twelve, the age at which American children are most confident of knowing precisely how a McDonald's is supposed to smell. I wouldn't have been surprised, in fact, if she had demonstrated an ability to distinguish by smell between a Burger King and a Wendy's — a hamburger chain she had once complimented, in her own way, as being "maybe not quite as junky as the others." Sarah has always had a good sniffer.

I would not want to leave the impression that Sarah had spent great hunks of her childhood waiting in line for Big Macs and Whopper burgers. By the standards of most American children, she was underexperienced as a consumer of fast food, partly because she was saddled with parents sufficiently biased toward slow food to believe that the hamburger should begin cooking after rather than before you ordered it. I would also not like to leave the impression that Sarah, whose reputation as an eater of considerable caution may have extended beyond our household, had just walked into an American-style fast-food joint on the Champs-Élysées because it was the only restaurant in Paris where she felt safe eating. In the first place, French waiters she had encountered during our stay in Uzès had been so attentive to her needs that she hadn't even bothered to learn the phrase *pas de légumes, s'il vous plaît*. In the second place, Sarah had never felt completely comfortable in establishments where a special order is necessary to get anything but the ornately dressed hamburgers the fast-food chains specialize in. She had always eaten her hamburgers just plain — except for what one fast-food menu I saw in Paris described as *"une touche de ketchup."* Sarah was not at Freetime as a casual consumer. She was there as a member of an inspection team.

I was on the team myself. In fact, I had organized it. I realize that making an inspection of American-style fast-food restaurants might sound like an odd way to spend one's time in Paris — rather like building a trip to Bavaria around a tour of American army NCO clubs. I had resolved to include such spots as Freetime and What a Burger and Dallas Burger in our tour of Paris landmarks, though, partly because of having seen a leisure-and-tourism section of *Le Monde* that devoted its front page to "fastefoude." It had an article about the proliferation of fast-food restaurants in France, a critical piece that awarded prizes to the best examples of fast food, and a large photograph of what looked to me like a Whopper burger. Abigail had spent a good deal of time translating the *Le Monde* article for me — a fact she had the grace not to mention as she bailed out of the inspection tour very early to join her mother in checking out the shops on the Rue du Faubourg Saint-Honoré.

Her departure left, in addition to Sarah and me, Simon Cherniavsky and his younger sister, Emma. I had thought that Simon and Emma might lend an international air to the panel: they were born in the

eastern United States, their parents are from England, they were attending a French boarding school,
and they had been to Texas. Since their mother,
Anne Willan, was running a well-known cooking
school in Paris called La Varenne, I had assumed
that for people of boarding-school age they had
broad gustatory experience — perhaps too broad for
the task at hand, it occurred to me on the way to the
Champs-Élysées, when Simon, who was thirteen,
told me that he liked squid.

Simon and Emma were along partly as translators,
although American English is used so resolutely in
fast-food establishments that even Freetime, which
promoted itself as an outfit that turns out American-
style fast food with a French touch, advertised one
of its special combinations as "Menu Frenchie." Also,
I thought Simon might serve as a guide, since I had
been told that he liked to go to the movies on the
Champs-Élysées, the center of the fast-food trade in
Paris. As he directed me toward a parking space that
was within striking distance of three or four burger
dispensers, I asked him what his favorite food was —
a bit concerned, after that squid remark, that he
might mention some gourmet wonder that would
bowl me over or cause Sarah to shudder. *"Pommes
frites,"* he said, to my relief. A French-fries man.
Very sound.

I was interested in how Sarah and Simon and

Emma would respond to what was served in Parisian fast-food restaurants — for instance, I welcomed the opportunity to see whether the various prizes that *Le Monde* had bestowed, such as the *prix du hamburger*, had been correctly awarded — but I was under no illusion about finding hamburgers that blotted out memories of my childhood in Kansas City, or French fries that rivaled the kind of freshly cut, triple-fried *pommes frites* that had helped persuade Sarah that France might be a place where one could avoid starvation after all. Fast-food outlets could never slow down that much. Aside from the food, I had a certain amount of simple curiosity about what, say, a Burger King on the Champs-Élysées would be like. The word "authentic" somehow seemed inappropriate, but I was sort of curious to see whether Paris fast-food joints were authentic.

Take the matter of lines. An essential of fast-food operations is a string of cash registers along a counter, each one of them manned by a cheerful teenager who fills the orders of the people lined up in front of him. Americans line up routinely, but in my experience all French lines are triangular — with the base of the triangle at the place where business is being conducted. (Italian lines tend to be oval.) The French are unable to maintain what the English would consider proper queue discipline, I've always thought, partly because they know that each person ahead of them in the line carries the potential of holding up the operation for an entire afternoon: any French functionary, whether charged with granting immigrant status or checking out volleyballs, is in danger at any moment of asking dozens of obscure questions and recording the answers in painful longhand on forms done in triplicate. I couldn't imagine that any fast-food outfit could afford to rent a store on the Champs-Élysées wide enough to accommodate more than one or two French lines. Also, it occurred to me that a customer who finally reached the head of the line at a French Burger King might ask for a couple of Whoppers, an order of fries, and a chocolate milkshake only to have the counterperson poise a scratchy quill pen over some exceedingly long form, look up sourly, and say, "Granmuzzer's maiden name?"

I don't mean I was surprised to hear that people in France — particularly young people — had taken up fast-food outlets like Burger King and Manhattan Burger not just as places to get a cheap meal but as places to hang out. In Western Europe, "America" — American places, American movie stars, American English — has become shorthand for a kind of zippy, cut-rate modernism. The cheap shirts displayed in an outdoor market in a small Italian village might well say on them, for no particular reason, HOLLYWOOD, or even SAN DIEGO. Just about any American who has traveled in Europe in the eighties has a story about being brought up short by the sight of an orange-and-black sweatshirt that says UNIVERSITY OF HARVARD or of a windbreaker that says TEAM TENNIS on it instead of TENNIS TEAM. Not long after François Mitterrand took power, his ministers expressed some resentment about Americanisms creeping into French — although it seemed to me that resentment would have been more understandable from Americans discovering that American English had become the *lingua schlocko* of Western Europe. I did not, however, approach the Champs-Élysées in a resentful mood, like one of those boosters of American culture who keep asking why French intellectuals can't spend a little more time studying American contributions to modern dance and a little less time celebrating the middle films of Jerry Lewis. I went to the fast-food outlets in Paris in the same spirit I might have gone to a baseball game in Tokyo: I just wanted to see if they had it right. Freetime didn't, we all decided. As a start, the hamburgers were rectangular. Team Tennis.

The hamburgers at Burger King were round. "This is more like an American hamburger," Emma said.

"It's exactly like an American hamburger," Sarah said. "Exactly."

Simon, a man who had eaten a squid, paused as if rolling over in his mind the sort of remark that might be appropriate to the occasion. Finally he said, "It seems more worthwhile."

Freetime, of course, was striving for a French version of American fast food. Burger King was striving to be Burger King, and that left no room for *herbes de Provence*. The outlet we were in could almost have been in America — except that it was in a cavernous basement room on the Champs-Élysées instead of in a freestanding building off a suburban double lane, and the sign on the wall read MAISON DU WHOPPER. The lines were linear. The people filling orders at the counter punched them out on those modern cash registers that simultaneously print out a bill and add it up and subtract the ingredients from inventory and, for all I know, record the counterperson's grandmother's maiden name. "This is getting close," I said.

Burger King had been the fast-food restaurant recommended to me by an American resident of Paris we happened to know — Matthew Pillsbury, who's a year or two younger than Sarah. Matthew's older brother apparently preferred a pizza joint called Slice, on the Boulevard Saint-Michel. Matthew spoke French in school and English at home — a staccato English, with French rhythms that caused me to miss a word now and then. He had spent a lot of summers in the upper Midwest, so he could shift from foot to foot in the gesture any ten-year-old American boy uses to mean "Maybe we could move on to the next subject." He could also blow air through his lips suddenly, without pursing them, like a Frenchman who is really saying, "But of course! It would be naïve to believe otherwise." In other words, he could be bilingual without saying anything.

When I asked Matthew why he preferred Burger King, he had said, "Not beefier."

"Not beefier?"

He nodded, ready to get on to the next subject.

"But why would you like it because it's *not* beefier?" I asked.

He sighed. Then he repeated the words, carefully and slowly: "Not beef ear!" He grabbed his ear to demonstrate, and added, "Some of them make their hamburgers out of beef ear."

"They do?" I said.

"Of course," Matthew said, as if repeating the obvious. "It's a scandal." He blew air out through his lips.

I suppose the notion that some fast-food places made their hamburgers from particularly strange cuts of beef may have had its origin in the publicity surrounding the efforts of McDonald's to cancel the franchise license of the McDonald's restaurants that had opened in Paris. McDonald's had claimed that the proprietor of the Paris outlets, Raymond Dayan, was not maintaining company standards in matters like cleanliness. Dayan claimed that McDonald's had underestimated the appeal of fast food in France — by the time we took our inspection tour, one Burger King outlet on the Champs-Élysées was doing more business than any other Burger King in the world — and, having made a deal with him for a royalty that proved to be low, was simply applying pressure in order to wiggle out of the contract. A judge in Chicago ruled for McDonald's, and Dayan changed the name of his outlets to O'Kitch. The standard sandwich of O'Kitch became a Kitchburger.

As names for Paris hamburgers go, "Kitchburger" was not out of the ordinary. The names of the dishes served by a fast-food restaurant in Paris are normally just variations on one English word — almost any English word. Freetime's word, of course, was "Hit." Dallas Burger, I found, offered a Big Dallas, a Dallas Burger, a Cheese Dallas, and a Fish Dallas. A place called Fun Burger had a Funny Burger, a Funny Cheese, and a Funny Fish. Sarah and Simon and Emma and I had our Kitchburger at the O'Kitch on the Champs-Élysées, just a block or two toward the Arc de Triomphe from Burger King. We were not impressed with the Kitchburger, but by then we had consumed quite a few hamburgers. At Freetime we had eaten two Hitfrenches, under the impression that we were trying a Hitburger the second time around. Simon, a young man of admirable thoroughness, had insisted on trying *pommes frites* everyplace we stopped. We were, to put it another way, no longer at our hungriest.

Still, I thought we ought to try What a Burger. As I remembered, *Le Monde* had given What a Burger the *prix du hamburger.* Simon didn't remember ever having seen a What a Burger outlet on the Champs-Élysées, so we headed for the Boulevard Saint-Michel and parked not far from Slice. As we walked up the boulevard, I didn't see any sign of a What a Burger. I did see an O'Kitch, and I realized from the ads outside it that the special double-decker that O'Kitch served was not the Kitchburger but the Bestkitch. That was what we should have had to compare with a burger like the Whopper. "We'd better try one," I said. "Fair's fair."

Emma said she wasn't really terribly hungry anymore. Sarah just shook her head. Simon and I tried a Bestkitch and shrugged. The double-deckers were beginning to run together. "Let's walk one more block," I said. "If we don't find What a Burger, we'll finish off with some ice cream — real French ice cream, assuming we don't come across a Baskin-Robbins with *trente et un parfums.*"

On the next block we found What a Burger. We ordered the double-decker, called a Super What. "Well?" I asked.

"I think it's the best," Emma said. "They deserve the prize."

Emma had taken a very small bite for her sampling. Even Simon seemed to be flagging. He took a rather modest bite, swallowed, and then shrugged. "Let's give it to them," he said. Sarah nodded, apparently willing to take Simon's word for it. I figured that we could go have some ice cream.

When Sarah and I got back to where we were staying, I informed Abigail that the inspection team had found just about what I had expected to find. If the French really put their minds to it, I said, they could make round hamburgers. Fast-food French fries in France as well as in America were, as I had expected, a slander on the real article. *Le Monde* had been correct when it awarded the *prix du hamburger* to What a Burger.

Abigail informed me that *Le Monde* had not awarded the *prix du hamburger* to What a Burger. I had remembered incorrectly. Burger King had won the *prix du hamburger*. *Le Monde* had given What a Burger an overall prize, stressing freshness of ingredients.

"Well, it's complicated," I said. "Also, what would the French know about such things?"

# 7

# The Last Babyfoot

BABYFOOT IS MY GAME. I know that the bare
statement of it carries no dash. I realize that there
are people who, when the subject of sports and
games comes up, prefer to say something like
"Squash is my sport" or even "My real game's polo,
of course." My real game is not polo, though, and
implying that it is, I've always assumed, is the sort
of pretense that could get me stepped on by a horse.

I suppose I could say that my sport is European in
origin, but somehow it doesn't seem European in
origin in the sense that, say, Alpine skiing is European in origin. One of the significant differences is
that Alpine skiing events do not take place in taverns. It's true, though, that the Germans may have
invented *babyfoot*; they call it something that sounds

like "foosball." It's still basically a European game. To the best of my memory, I started playing it in Italy, where it is known as *calcetto* or *calcio balilla*. But I've always referred to it by its French name, *babyfoot*, perhaps because it's one of the few French words — *sweater*, *drugstore*, and *smoking* are among the others — that I can mispronounce with some authority. I don't much like the most common American name, "table soccer." That conjures up something done on a bridge table — a game like Parcheesi, maybe, played by people who have just come in from squash or polo. My sport is nothing like that.

I'll admit that the name "table soccer" is a start toward describing *babyfoot*. The table, which is actually more like an open rectangular box on legs, is about the size of the horizontal part of a pinball machine — a comparison that may come to mind because there is often a pinball machine just a few feet away. The floor of the box has the markings of a soccer field, and there's a goal at each end. Hidden somewhere in the box's innards are ten solid white balls slightly smaller than Ping-Pong balls; they become available with the insertion of a coin and disappear when they go into a goal. The balls are propelled by "men" — blue men or red men, depending on which team they're on — that extend down from eight rods running across the box. The men, each about the size of a large cigar, are made of cast iron or hard plastic, and on a well-designed machine they suggest the figure of a soccer player, in an abstract sort of way. The rod nearest each goal has only one man, the plucky goalkeeper. Two defensemen are on the rod just in front of him, facing a three-man rod that is ordinarily the main scoring threat of the opposition. In the middle of the table, the two teams face each other with four-man rods. *Babyfoot* is customarily played with two people on a side — one person handling the goalie and the defensemen, his partner taking care of the three-man attack rod and the four-man rod in the center. A skilled player can slide the ball over from one of the men on his rod to another. He can pass, say, from the goalie to one of the defensemen, or even to one of the men controlled by his partner. At least one longtime player of *babyfoot* can pass from a defenseman back toward his own goal, and slam the ball with his goalie — his goalie! — in a way that propels it with astonishing velocity the entire length of the table and into the opponents' goal. I am that player.

*Babyfoot* was my game long before we whiled away — "wasted," Mrs. Alec Tweedie would have said — those evenings at the soccer bar in Uzès. In the way that people sometimes recall foreign travels by a particularly splendid meal or some comical misadventure ("Remember, it was that town where the Italian policeman you asked for directions to the cathedral somehow got the idea that you wanted to buy his shoes"), Alice and I sometimes punctuate our recollections of foreign travels with memorable *babyfoot* contests. She happens to play a capable forward game. I can remember the time in the mid-sixties when, while driving through the Dolomites, we spotted a *babyfoot* machine standing right in the tiny square of a mountain village, and we stopped to play two Italian boys who couldn't have been older than nine or ten. (Without meaning to make excuses, I might add that the contest was a lesson in how an out-of-towner, playing outdoors for the first time, can be tricked by clever and perhaps not completely scrupulous opponents into taking the side of the table where the glare of the sun on the field is quite distracting.) We've played *babyfoot* in Spain and we've played it in Mexico. When I think of the pleasures of a provincial French town, the picture that often comes into my mind is that café in Uzès — photographs of the local soccer team on the wall, a few outdoor tables where men gather over glasses of the stuff the French persist in drinking, and, off in the back, four people playing a fierce game of *babyfoot*.

My memories of *babyfoot* in America are mainly of people wondering what in the world it could possibly be. "You play baby *what*?" someone might say, just after he has spent fifteen or twenty minutes discussing his backhand. For a few years in the mid-seventies, though, it appeared that *babyfoot*, which had never had great success finding space among the pinball machines and table shuffleboard and pool tables in American bars, was finally catching on in the United States. The new popularity was gained largely through the efforts of Lee Peppard, of Missoula, Montana, who had started out at nineteen promoting miniature-golf tournaments and had then turned to coin-operated billiards. Peppard had been running a sort of combination tavern and billiard parlor in Missoula when he decided that foosball, as *babyfoot* was then called in America, was the jackpot. He eventually called it Tournament Soccer, since the cornerstone of his efforts to promote the game and sell machines — he had formed his own company to sell machines that were constructed in Taiwan — was a series of tournaments. Within a few years it was not unusual for Peppard to hold a tournament that awarded a quarter of a million dollars in prize money — although the competitors still had to feed the machines with their own quarters.

As the tournaments proliferated, there came to be people identified in the press as professional foosball players. Peppard insisted that *babyfoot* was an authentic sport, comparable to bowling rather than to pinball. I couldn't have agreed more. It's true that most sports are not coin-operated, but, as foosball pros on tour would ask the skeptical, what is the essential difference between dropping a quarter in a slot and paying a greens fee at a golf course? The culmination of Peppard's efforts to win acceptance for *babyfoot* as a legitimate sporting event came in September of 1975, when *Sports Illustrated* ran a piece headlined "A REAL FIRST-CLASS PROFESSIONAL SPORT." It's true that the headline was within quotation marks, and it's true that the quotation was from Peppard. Still, I think that players of the game took the *Sports Illustrated* coverage as confirmation of what they had been saying all along. "The fact is that table soccer has all the elements of a truly legitimate major sport — strategies, highly refined techniques, and an emphasis on speed, reflexes, and coordination," Jim Congdon, then president of the World Table Soccer Association, wrote in *RePlay*, a magazine that covers the jukebox-and-coin-games industry. "This makes table soccer enjoyable not only as light entertainment but also as aggressive competition, susceptible to high degrees of skill." My sentiments exactly.

The boom never spread completely across the country — it never got to New York, for instance — and it lasted only a few years. In the late seventies, table soccer was gradually driven out of bars by video games. In the view of Ed Adlum, the publisher of *RePlay*, "it just couldn't make decent money unless there was a big promotion." Peppard's promotional efforts came to a noisy end. In what turned out to be a sort of symbolic finale, he organized a tournament extravaganza of *babyfoot* and a few other games in Chicago, and some of the prizewinners found that the element of rebound, which is significant in *babyfoot*, extended to their prize checks. "That was the end of table soccer," Ed Adlum has said. "Lee Peppard is a great promoter — he could sell water in a flood — but table soccer was a blip in our industry."

I have to admit that my hopes for *babyfoot*'s acceptance in America had been limited from the start. I never thought that the people who seemed to talk a lot about their ground strokes would start discussing how they were progressing in their efforts to master some of the *babyfoot* moves mentioned in the *Sports Illustrated* piece — the Texas Pull Shot, for instance, or the Louisiana Shuffle Defense. I had more or less resigned myself to playing *babyfoot* in foreign countries and being patient whenever someone in the United States said, "You play baby *what*?"

At some point in the early eighties, though, it began to occur to me that I seemed to be seeing fewer *babyfoot* machines in foreign countries. I still found the occasional bar where — usually in a sort of storage room, shared with plastic soft-drink cartons and some pasteboard boxes of bar supplies — a *babyfoot* stood ready for the astonishing goalie shot. In a lot of bars, though, the *babyfoot* table seemed to have been snuffed out by video games, which had hopped the Atlantic Ocean and were catching on in Western Europe like a bad weed. The apparent decline in *babyfoot* opportunities was particularly distressing to me because I had waited years for Abigail and Sarah to grow old enough to hold their own in adult competition, giving us a full complement of players right in the family. In the summer of 1985 we came across only one *babyfoot* in all of Florence, in a small café across from the church of Santa Croce. As Alice and I and Sarah prepared to return to Italy the next summer — Abigail wasn't able to join us, but we were bringing along a school friend of Sarah's named Alix as goalie for the blue team — I was concerned about whether we'd find any *babyfoot* at all.

As it happened, Sarah, who was then fourteen, seemed to have inherited her mother's talent at the forward game. In fact, she had developed a spectacular version of what I assume *Sports Illustrated* meant by the Texas Pull Shot. Using the three men on the attack rod, she would employ an outside man to rake the ball from the edge of the field toward her center man, who would drill it past the goalie with a power that seemed remarkable coming from someone who did not have the appearance normally associated with what baseball people call a slugger. When we arrived in Italy, I harbored some fantasies about a few surprises that Sarah and I could provide to a couple of overconfident Italian *calcetto* whizzes — maybe that pair from the Dolomite village, although they must be even better now that they're old enough to see over the table. I realize that there are parents who believe that Sarah, rather than spending her summer in the back of saloons playing *babyfoot*, should have been at, say, tennis camp. I realize that in the matter of parents' responsibility to pass on some appreciation for the culture of the Western world there is an argument for raising a child in a home where Santa Croce has never even once been referred to as "the big church near the *babyfoot* bar." Still, I couldn't help imagining the looks on the faces of the local champs when Sarah's attack shot slammed into the goal. I had a feeling that *babyfoot* was Sarah's game.

We were staying near a town called Borgo a Buggiano, about forty-five minutes from Florence. The likely bar in Borgo, it seemed to me, was a place called the Caffè Garibaldi. On the side it had a sort of garden where some of the men of the town gathered to have a glass of wine and play cards. Three or four extra chairs — the colored plastic chairs common to outdoor cafés in Italian towns — faced the street right at the curb, presumably for the convenience of traditionalists who didn't feel comfortable drinking more than two or three feet away from motorbike exhausts. On the wall were a couple of posters and the season's standings for a local amateur soccer league — an indication of interest in the field version of my sport as well as a particular treat for an English speaker, since the Italian word for amateurs, *dilettanti,* conjures up a picture of twenty-two people wearing ascots while they kick a ball around and discuss, say, what they think of the latest French film or how their new interest in ballet has forced them to give up some promising attempts at abstract sculpture. I noticed that the Garibaldi had an anteroom. I peeked. Two pinball machines and two video games.

I tried what seemed to be the most substantial bar in town, a place called the Caffè Centrale. It was a lot roomier than the Garibaldi, and it had two full-sized pool tables that looked as if they might be considered too handsome to use. On the wall were pictures of pool players and bicyclists. The Caffè Centrale, in other words, could pass muster as a sporting bar. There was a small second room, obviously the place where coins were dropped. It held two pinball machines and a video game that featured a Western bad guy shooting at a train. At the Remo, a much smaller place down the street, the only machine was a pinball called Double Crown. I hadn't actually expected much from the Remo, but I was optimistic about a place called the Bar Sport Biago, which, as far as I could gather from the photographs and trophies on the wall, sponsored its own soccer team. The Bar Sport Biago had a video game, a pinball called Miss Americana, and a pinball called Earth, Wind & Fire. It had no *babyfoot*. No bar in Borgo a Buggiano had a *babyfoot*.

I found one the next day at an amusement arcade on the main street. In fact, the arcade had two *babyfoots*. It also had a dozen or so video games, a couple of pinball machines, a jukebox stuffed with loud rock records, and a clientele that looked like the Tuscan road company of *Grease*. I suppose I would have played at the arcade as a last resort, but I didn't have any realistic expectation of being accompanied by the rest of my party. I took to looking around nearby cities. In Montecatini, I could find only one *babyfoot* — in an amusement arcade tackier and noisier than the one in Borgo. Pescia seemed to have no *babyfoots*. Even Lucca, which I have held up as a model town for hanging around, did not seem to include among its many charms a single *babyfoot*.

## The Last Babyfoot

As if all that weren't discouragement enough, I met an Italian woman who seemed to take some pride in keeping up with what was happening culturally in Italy as well as in several other countries, and when I mentioned my interest in *calcetto* she said simply, "But it's finished."

Then we found ourselves in Florence one day, and in discussing the great sights of the city, I thought of the church of Santa Croce. Alice had some errands to do, but Sarah and Alix and I took a walk toward the church, accompanied by a visiting friend named Wayne, who lives in France part of the year and had assured us that he was capable of performing adequately as a fourth. ("I was playing *babyfoot* when you were in baby shoes.") I had no trouble at all finding the bar. The room that had held the *babyfoot* seemed unchanged. In it were some beer cases and a couple of M & M cartons and two propane canisters and some cases of mineral water and three videos and a pinball called Star God and a pinball called Time Machine. In a roomy area near the beer cases stood the *babyfoot* table I remembered — what I had come to think of as the last *babyfoot*. It was occupied.

Two young men were playing a ferocious game of singles, switching their hands madly to get at the appropriate rod, slamming the ball so hard that it sometimes jumped right out of the box onto the floor. We didn't have much time before we were due to meet Alice some distance away. I realized that we might have found the last *babyfoot* at a time when we were unable to play it. I must have revealed my impatience to the players, because after five or ten minutes one of them looked over to me and said, in excellent English, that he and his friend were about finished. A couple of minutes later, when their game had ended, he asked if we wanted to play them one game before we took over the table. I supposed he meant Wayne and me. Without hesitation I said, with a gesture toward Sarah, "Maybe you'd like to play me and my little girl." Sarah gave me the look she sometimes flashes just before she says "Oh, Daddy!" but I couldn't tell whether it had been provoked by my suggestion or by my referring to her (for strategic reasons) as a little girl. The young man I had spoken to translated for his friend, who chuckled.

"Be careful of her," I said as we stepped up to the table. "She's got fast hands and she's mean."

I won't say we won. I'd like to say we won. If Wayne and Alix and Sarah weren't available to correct me, I suppose I would say we won. I will say, though, that we acquitted ourselves magnificently. The two young men were fantastic players; the English speaker later told me that his friend had often played in *calcetto* tournaments in southern Italy, which is apparently a better place to look for *baby-foots* in bars. They passed to each other casually. At times they hit the ball so hard that I actually couldn't see it whiz past my men. Still, after a couple of points Sarah scooped the ball toward her middle attack man and smashed it past the opposing goalie, causing the young man who was responsible for defending the goal to look somewhat embarrassed.

"Fast and mean," I reminded him.

Then, after a few more points we needn't go into, something happened that I think I'll always recall when I hear that phrase "Great Moments in Sports." One of my defensemen stopped the ball and pushed it back toward our own goal. I had already pulled back the goalie to start his shot, and the swing forward connected with the pass perfectly. The ball went the length of the field — the length of the field! — into the opposing goal. After that, I thought, they could score as many points as they wanted to. And they did.

When we returned from Italy, I learned from the people at *RePlay* that a *babyfoot*-manufacturing company called Dynamo had been holding some tournaments around the country and that a new outfit called Striker was planning an ambitious tournament in Long Beach, California, over Labor Day weekend. One of the organizers of the Long Beach tournament told me, in fact, that it would include the first ceremony of the American Table Soccer Federation Hall of Fame. As a beginning, the Hall of Fame was planning to induct nine players and three manufacturers — including Lee Peppard, who had turned from table soccer to organizing electronic-dart tournaments in the Pacific Northwest. I was encouraged by the activity, but I knew we'd continue to think of *babyfoot* as something we play in foreign countries. The future looked brighter on that score, since I knew that we simply had to go farther south in Italy to find proper soccer bars. I only regretted that I hadn't asked the young man in Florence about specific bars in the south. I'm sure he would have provided some. I've found that in any sport athletes of tournament caliber tend to be generous about sharing information with their colleagues.

# 8

# Full Basket

WHEN A WOMAN I KNOW named Nathalie Waag told me that she was planning to take in a few boarders at a time for a holiday she called Eight Days in Provence, she also made it clear in advance that in her view a day in Provence consists basically of going to a market and then eating what you managed to get there. That made sense to me. There is no better way to spend a morning in Provence than to go to a market in a town square, where farm couples have set up small tables with what they picked just before dawn, and where huge trucks have opened side panels to reveal that they are in fact butcher shops or shoe stores; there is no better way to spend an evening in Provence than to eat the dinner that somebody like Nathalie has made out of the contents of the market basket. I can see having a swim or taking in a façade or two late in the afternoon, but I would consider those strictly side activities. In fact, until *The Hanging Around Guide to France* and its companion volumes are published, I think all European towns should be required to announce on their city-limit signs which day is market day, the way American towns sometimes announce the time and place of the regular Kiwanis lunch.

The summer that Nathalie launched her new business we were staying for a while just outside a Provençal town called Saint-Rémy, in an area sometimes known as the Heart of Provence. The place we were renting was only a few kilometers from what I thought of as the heart of the heart — Maillane, the home village of Frédéric Mistral, who won the Nobel Prize in 1904 for poems he had written in Provençal, the traditional language of the region. Mistral's devotion to Provençal was so complete, I read in a guidebook, that he refused to speak French — a position I could sympathize with, particularly when I was trying to tell a shopkeeper something that seemed to call for a verb in the conditional tense. I had no way of knowing whether the villagers of Maillane used to say to each other (in French), "Good old Fred — sticks to his guns" or "Let's duck behind the fountain or Freddy's going to

spot us and lay that Provençal rap on us again."
Either way, I told Abigail and Sarah whenever we
passed the Mistral homestead on one of our evening
bike rides, you had to admire anyone as gloriously
pigheaded as Frédéric Mistral. I told them that we
were fortunate indeed to be so close to what we took
to calling "Freddy's place" — the little museum that
had been made out of his house. Sarah thought that
a more interesting matter of proximity was that we
were only about eighty-five miles from a place called
Aqualand, which, according to a brochure she had
somehow come across, had four separate water
slides, one of them called Anaconda. If I ever got
lost in the desert, I think I'd like to have Sarah with
me: she'd find a water slide.

We were also only thirty or forty miles from the
farmhouse Nathalie Waag had near Bonnieux, and
I saw the proximity as an opportunity to go marketing
with someone I knew to be a formidable gatherer of
foodstuffs. I had once seen her in action — examining artichokes like a jeweler examining a second-
hand diamond, chatting up the elderly farm woman
who happened to bring in the best mixture of baby
lettuce every market day, fixing some vegetable man
with the narrowed eyes of a customs inspector as
she asked him precisely when the vegetables were
picked. I've never been able to get much out of an
artichoke examination myself. And even though I've

read all the instructions about how to gauge the freshness of a fish by looking him in the eye, the fish I eyeball look pretty noncommittal. I'm still waiting for the first one to lower his eyes in guilty knowledge of how long he has been out of the water.

I knew Nathalie to be the sort of person who could look a *rouget* in the eye and get something out of the experience. Also, she obviously had a wide knowledge of which Provençal specialties could be found where — vital information for short-time visitors, since among the suggestions of mine that had been ignored by the Ministry of Tourism was the suggestion that each French town list on its city-limit sign, just below the announcement of which day is market day, any local delicacies that the residents are particularly proud of ("The bakery right on the square has an excellent version of *fougasse,* a Provençal specialty that is somewhere between bread and pizza. We think you'd enjoy it"). I couldn't really complain about the food we had been eating in Provence. We were regularly coming home from the market — the Wednesday market in Saint-Rémy, say, or the Saturday market in Arles — with three or four different kinds of lettuce, raspberries, cherries, rice from the Camargue, *saucisson* from the Ardèche, two or three different kinds of pâté, four or five different kinds of *chèvre*, a selection of olives, a farm-grown chicken, a couple of pizzas, and half a dozen Vietnamese spring rolls. Every morning I would bicycle into the village, to a baker named Mme Rosa, for *pain de brioche* and peasant bread and croissants. A Provençal restaurant only fifteen or twenty minutes away served an astonishing *pistou* — a Provençal specialty that bears the same resemblance to vegetable soup that a Greek wedding celebration bears to a bridge-club tea. Still, the thought that I could be completely unaware of some legendary local cheese practically at our doorstep or some brilliant purveyor of *bourride* just down the road was always with me.

❧

Several years before, Nathalie had operated a restaurant in Vence for a while, but she said that it was something she got into more or less by accident and got out of with great relief. She likes to shop and she likes to cook and she likes to sit around the dinner table with friends, but she doesn't take to bookkeeping. Just after her restaurant closed, she happened to meet Alice Waters, the proprietor of Chez Panisse, in Berkeley, who occupies the same role in what is sometimes called the New California Cuisine that Emma Goldman once occupied in the old American anarchism. They discovered that they had a lot in common — particularly after they had spent some time at Nathalie's place in Bonnieux going to markets.

Eventually, one of Nathalie's sons worked for a

while at Chez Panisse as a salad chef. Then her other son got a job there; his job was to go to market. Nathalie became part of what amounts to an East Bay–Provence alliance. Kermit Lynch, the wine importer closest to Chez Panisse and the restaurants that spun off it, specializes in the wines of Provence; the proprietors of one winery he deals with, near Bandol, act as sort of French country cousins for any of the East Bay food people who are in the area. Richard Olney, who grew up in a small town about eighty miles from Sioux City but has lived for many years in the South of France, is the cookbook author who had the most influence on Alice Waters and some of the other East Bay chefs — which means, I suppose, that the New California Cuisine, like a good bit of the California population, can trace its origins to Iowa. Like Olney and a number of other people who have become particularly knowledgeable about Provençal food, Nathalie is from somewhere else. Until she was eighteen or so, she lived in Switzerland — an experience she discusses in the tone a Manhattan museum curator might use to discuss his boyhood in Tulsa.

When Nathalie decided to offer her Eight Days in Provence package, she was in California visiting her son; she simply put up a notice at Chez Panisse and a notice at Kermit Lynch's retail wine store, not far away. The potential guests sorted themselves out when they met Nathalie to ask about details. When some people asked whether tennis facilities were convenient to the house, Nathalie realized that they would not be suitable for her; when they saw the look on her face in response, they must have realized that her notion of Eight Days in Provence would not be suitable for them.

Monday, the day I joined Nathalie and her guests, is market day in Cavaillon — the place the melon was named after — but Nathalie, who considers the Cavaillon market nothing special, was in the habit of going to Forcalquier instead. Although she didn't keep a rigid schedule, she told me, there were markets she normally visited on certain days of the week. On Sunday, there was a market at L'Isle-sur-la-Sorgue noted not just for food but also for antiques. On Tuesday or Thursday, Nathalie usually went to the market in Aix-en-Provence. On Wednesday, she often went to Saint-Rémy. Saturday was market day in Apt, a city only a few miles from Bonnieux. On Friday, Nathalie and her guests sometimes gave up marketing in favor of a trip to a winery not far from Les Baux and a long lunch at a restaurant in Paradou that still serves the traditional Provençal Friday meal of *aïoli* — garlic mayonnaise accompanied by cod and snails and potatoes and vegetables to scoop it up with. In Provence a club can be said to be holding an *aïoli* in the way a club in Texas can be said to be holding a barbecue, and the word has the same sort of strong regional identification. In an antique stall at the Arles market late one Saturday morning, at about the time I was beginning to have second thoughts about whether I had chosen the right one of a dozen or so different types of sausage, I saw copies of an old Provençal newspaper that was called *L'Aïoli*. It was one of the moments when I realized that I was probably going to eat pretty well in Provence no matter how many delicacies escaped my notice: people who can name a newspaper *The Garlic Mayonnaise* are my kind of folks.

Nathalie liked to go to Forcalquier partly because it provided a change of scenery — it's on the northeast edge of Provence, in the area sometimes known as the Basses-Alpes — and partly because there were vendors there who weren't found in the other markets she visited. Some of the vendors were from cities farther to the north and east, like Digne. There were also a number of counterculture vendors. Apparently, some areas in the South of France had a great influx of young dropouts after the political turmoil in Paris in 1968, and Forcalquier turned out to be a place that many of them never left — giving the market a broad supply of organic vegetables and stone-ground flour and other staples of what the unsympathetic might think of as hippie fodder.

### Full Basket

On the Monday I joined Nathalie in Forcalquier, the people staying at her house for Eight Days in Provence were two amiable couples from Oakland. Among them was a periodontist who took careful notes for a journal of eating he was preparing for his patients — a journal that, I am pleased to say, had nothing to do with what foods would be beneficial for oral hygiene but concentrated instead on what foods had made him particularly happy. Before we started our wanderings through the market, Nathalie pointed out an outdoor café where we would all meet when the vendors began to pack up their wares around noon. Nathalie was shopping for lunch as well as dinner, since she always showed up at the agreed-upon café with a picnic. I did not, as it turned out, get any lessons in artichoke examination by watching her gather food for two meals. She picked what she needed by judgment that had become too natural to put into words. When I asked her how it was possible to distinguish among so many vendors of *chèvre* — every one of them was displaying *chèvres* of various freshness, arranged like well-trained platoons — she looked surprised, and then explained, "You look at the cheese."

The Forcalquier market was the sort of market that spilled out through the town, so that when it seemed to be over you might come across two or three more squares filled with garlic vendors and cheese tables and chicken dealers and fishmongers and flower stalls and at least one fruit-and-vegetable dealer who unpacked his avocados from a box that said MISSION PRODUCE, INC., OXNARD CA 93034. Nathalie picked up a guinea fowl and some green beans and some shallots for dinner. For the café picnic she bought *fougasse* with anchovies and olive oil, some pizza with wild mushrooms, and two or three *pains bagnats* — a *pain bagnat* being, more or less, a *salade niçoise* in a bun. For dessert she bought some *chèvre* and some *brousse,* which is a kind of cheese made with ewe's milk. To avoid problems about bringing her own lunch to a café, Nathalie had picked a place that did not serve food. As we all tore into the picnic, the waiter didn't look irritated — just envious.

Everyone at the table agreed that the market had been splendid. Forcalquier had an almost rustic quality to it — a great contrast, Nathalie said, to Aix-en-Provence, where the Tuesday picnic would be held in a café on the sophisticated Cours Mirabeau and the dessert would be from a chocolate shop that is known in Paris. Nathalie likes variety. She got into the habit of visiting what is actually a rather small market in Saint-Rémy on Wednesdays, she said, partly because of the charm of the town and partly because of a bakery that sells fish-shaped pastry filled with *brandade de morue.*

"*Brandade de morue!*" I said. *Brandade de morue* — a sort of paste made from salt cod and potatoes and garlic — happened to be one of my favorite dishes.

Nathalie said that it was available from a baker named Mme Rosa.

"But Mme Rosa's our baker!" I said. "I never realized!"

Nathalie shrugged, as if everyone knew about Mme Rosa's *feuilleté de brandade de morue.* I suppose it did seem rather obvious. What would be inside fish-shaped pastry — apples and cinnamon? Nathalie said it was about time to get back to Bonnieux. Her guests were planning to spend the late afternoon writing postcards and playing *petanque*, the local version of *boules*, and looking forward to what Nathalie was going to concoct from the guinea fowl and the shallots and the green beans and whatever else she had around the house. I was ready to head back toward Saint-Rémy. Although my market basket was already rather heavy, I thought I might stop at Saint-Étienne, where farmers who have gathered to sell their produce to distributors will part with small lots before the commercial market officially opens. Also, since I hadn't really bought anything to take back for Alice and the girls, I thought it might be a good idea to make a stop at Mme Rosa's.

# 9

# Full Italian Basket

THIS HAPPENED just half an hour after I had arrived at the Rialto market in Venice, very early one morning in July, a year after I spent some time in Provençal markets with Nathalie Waag. I was, at the time, watching boxes of squash with their flowers still on being unloaded from a barge. I was also half listening to an aria being hummed by a nearby fishmonger, who was arranging his display of *rospi* and other *pesci freschissimi* from the Adriatic. (A *rospo* has a set of pointed little teeth, giving Venetian fishmongers the opportunity to liven up rows of inert sea creatures by bending around an occasional specimen's tail and hooking it into the mouth.) A couple of fruit sellers were engaged in what I took to be a ritualistic mock disparagement of each other's displays. Another fishmonger was whistling another song. Suddenly I heard myself exclaim, "Of course! It's Kansas City!"

I suppose I'd better explain that. Over the hundreds of years that visitors from abroad have been attracted to Venice, they must have responded to its charms in a great variety of ways, but it's probably not common to hear them say, "You know, it reminds me a bit of Kansas City." The reason I was an exception goes back to my infatuation with markets. I am a sucker for not just the weekly market in the square of a small French town but the wholesale city market that caters to people like produce distributors and restaurant proprietors. The section of the Venice market I was strolling through was like that, except that the characteristic city-market sound of trucks in low gear was missing. I even like going to the market in England, where a foreign visitor runs the risk of becoming dispirited at the thought of what the vegetables being bought have in store for them. Driving in the rural United States, I have never passed a market without stopping. I feel the way about them the way I used to feel about roadside zoos — except now, of course, I'm at the wheel. In New York, I'm a regular at the Saturday market in Union Square, where farmers come from upstate and New Jersey and Pennsylvania to sell fruits and vegetables to miraculously cheerful New Yorkers;

when the legendary baker from Yonkers arrives at her usual spot, rather late in the morning as market time goes, I stand patiently with the other devotees as she and her husband unload a car that contains a steaming tray of something too good to be called cheesecake. I like the couple from Yonkers — I like market people and the market atmosphere in general — but I'd stand in line to buy that cheesecake from someone who had the personality of my old Latin teacher.

The appeal of markets is so obvious to me that I never thought it necessary to explain the sources of my interest. In fact, I long ago admitted in print that when I'm visiting some friends we have in the west of England, spending a good deal of time gathering provisions that include some runner-bean chutney and Cheshire cheese, I'm completely baffled as to why so many of the other tourists are at the Tower of London or the Changing of the Guard instead of at Barnstaple Market. I have always understood, of course, that my interest in markets began when I was a child in Kansas City: I used to go to the city market once a summer with my father. When he opened his first grocery store, my father took for granted the necessity of going to the city market every day to pick out his own produce, and despite growing evidence over the years that other grocers were managing quite nicely by placing their orders on the telephone, he never gave up the custom. When people he met learned that the alarm went off at four in the morning in our house, they tended to say to my father, "Well, I guess you get used to it after a while," and he always said, "No, not really."

To me, going to the market was an annual adventure rather than a daily chore. The market people seemed particularly animated and jolly; a number of them carried on running repartees with my father that had become well polished over the years. The closest thing Kansas City had to the European ethnic neighborhoods of an Eastern city was a small Italian community on the northeast side, and my only contact with it as a child was at the city market; a lot of people who pressed apples on me or joked with my father about the quality of the green beans had names like Palermo or Cipolla. My memory of the details of those annual visits is so flawed that I distinctly remember shivering in the early-morning cold as I waited for my father to pull the car out of the garage — nobody has ever been cold in Kansas City in the summer, early in the morning or at any other time — but the total impression obviously became the model for markets I visited years after that. However hazy the details of the model, I knew that somehow no other wholesale market I visited — not even renowned places like Les Halles in Paris or Covent Garden in London — completely fulfilled my vision of what a city market is supposed to be. Then, in Venice, as I listened to the fishmongers' songs and watched the banter of the fruit sellers, I finally realized what markets in other parts of the world had lacked in reaching toward the Kansas City ideal: Italians.

I wish I could report that Italy, with its almost unique capacity for having every stall manned by an Italian, has only markets that the most demanding market trotter would find faultless. I did, in fact, run across a number of foodstuffs that would inspire any vendor to break out in song. In Greve, a market town in the Chianti Classico wine country, south of Florence, I stood in front of the cheese vendor and polished off some fresh parmesan that made me wonder what I had seen in the Cheshire at Barnstaple. A number of markets had fruit so spectacular that even my father would have had difficulty pretending to assume that it was last week's leftovers. But for every stand selling cheese or salami or vegetables in the small-town weekly markets, there were at least half a dozen stalls selling dresses or blue jeans or detergent or mop handles. If I had heard myself exclaiming something half an hour after I arrived at the first weekly market I went to that summer — the Monday market in San Casciano, near Florence — it would have been "I don't come to markets to buy scrub brushes."

It's not that I have anything against markets that don't concentrate on foodstuffs. One of the markets I most enjoyed walking around, a monthly market held on the grounds of a temple in Kyoto, was not dominated by food — although, now that I think of it, some of the particularly mysterious items I saw on display there could have been edible. But what I found offered for sale at San Casciano was mostly the sort of thing you might encounter at a discount store in a strip shopping center. I had arrived at about eight in the morning, eager and a little bit hungry. By eight-thirty I was rather discouraged. Then, in the one row of stalls devoted to food, I came across a man standing behind a hog.

He had just opened one of those small market trucks that fold down on one side to provide a show-case and a high counter. In the case was an entire roasted hog — entire except for its head, that is, which was displayed on the counter. The man had a huge knife, and he cut pork off any part of the hog that struck the customer's fancy. He sold meat from the hog by the kilo. He also made sandwiches out of the hog and sold them. Presumably, at the end of the day the hog would be gone, and the next week the vendor would come back with another hog. His presence cheered me. I had a sandwich, and I was cheered even more. The market seemed more like a market. Also, I admire a man who can make an industry out of a hog.

Eight o'clock was actually rather late for me to have arrived. I associate markets, particularly wholesale food markets, with the early hours. When my father finally got out of the grocery business and spent a year or so looking around for another line of work, he sometimes went down to the city market to play in the pitch game that formed when the main activity of the day was over, and (probably to the relief of his children, who found it awkward to have the one father around who wasn't obviously employed) that meant that he left our house at around the time the other fathers were leaving for work. Any place I've been to the market, which means just about any place I've been, seems different in the early-morning hours. In Venice, the contrast between early morning and the rest of the day was particularly vivid. On the morning I went early to the market on the Rialto, I walked across Venice at about six, and I stopped to count the people in the Piazza San Marco. Besides me, there were seven. Three were sweeping, and two were putting out café chairs. I hardly need to say what the two others were doing: he was taking a picture of her in front of the Basilica.

The fact that market people keep odd hours may be one of the reasons that they don't seem to observe conventions having to do with when it is appropriate to eat what. In that respect, I think they are challenged as an occupational group only by army cooks, who are always strolling around the mess-hall kitchen dipping a spoon into a bowl of something you wouldn't have expected them to be eating just then. If an Italian fishmonger or a French butcher walks into a market café at six in the morning, there is no way to know whether he's going to order coffee or a ham sandwich or onion soup or scrambled eggs or just cognac.

When it comes to being set in their ways, market people can't be compared to army cooks or anybody else. It's a trait I've always found admirable — or at least familiar. When a vegetable vendor is adding up my purchases on the paper he's about to wrap them in, I am never tempted to ask why he doesn't use the cash register behind him; that would be as useful as having asked my father why he didn't just phone in his produce order. A few days after visiting the market in Venice, I spent an early morning at the Central Market in Florence, a collection of retail stalls in a great pile of a nineteenth-century building near the center of the city. As splendid as the building was, I wasn't surprised to read in a guidebook that it sat empty for years because the market people, then in open stalls closer to the Arno, refused to move into it. Those in charge of Florence in the late nineteenth century did what city administrators have customarily had to do in order to force vendors into a new market: they tore down the old one.

Florence is a meat-and-potatoes town — especially meat. I found the ground floor of the Central Market to be more dominated by butcher shops than any market I've ever been in except the markets I strolled through once on a trip to Argentina. The Central Market had an entire second floor of vegetable stalls, but in Argentina I sometimes had difficulty finding any vegetables at all. Argentina, of course, has a national obsession with beef. In a market in Buenos Aires, beef is often cheaper than chicken. It is said that an Argentine entering a restaurant always studies the menu very carefully and then says, "Steak." One woman I met in Buenos Aires assured me that her in-laws, whom she described as "very Argentine," sincerely believe that all fish is poison. In an Argentine *parilla,* or grill, it is not unusual to have a mixed plate of chorizo, blood sausage, and sweetbreads as an appetizer, and then move on to the main course of meat. As if the feeling for meat were not pervasive enough, the school uniform in Argentina consists of a white cotton coat, so a visitor who walks by a school just as the children have been dismissed can get the impression that he is walking down the street among hundreds of tiny butchers.

When I stopped by the only café in the Central Market of Florence, I found that its specialty was a meat sandwich — veal, the day I was there. The sandwich maker carved slices from a large piece of veal that was sitting on a platter in an inch or two of juice. Then he chopped the slices into finer pieces. Then he took a bun, sliced it in two, placed both halves in the veal platter inner side down, and, with an index finger on each half, submerged them in the juice. Then he packed up the dripping bun with the veal, added what appeared to be about a quarter of a cup of salt, and handed it over. Breakfast.

I didn't have a veal sandwich myself. I was temporarily full from the effects of two or three *bocconcini*. A *bocconcino* is a mozzarella cheese about the size of an egg. If you play your market stalls right, it's a buffalo-milk mozzarella cheese about the size of an egg. Nobody can criticize it as food that is inappropriate for eating at six or seven in the morning: it's soft, it's mild, and it's absolutely oozing milk. In Italy I adopted it as my market snack, although I have to say that at the Central Market in Florence I eventually backed it up with some of the café's bean soup. In fact, the more *bocconcini* I ate, the more I came around to the view that, upon examination, the paragons we remember from childhood never had the perfection in reality that they have in our memories. Even today, I would guess, *bocconcini* are not available in Kansas City.

# 10

## The Playing Fields of Mott Street

I SUSPECT THAT MY GUEST from another land — an old Canadian friend called Fraser — left New York thinking that the entire purpose of our walk had been to lure him into the humiliation of being defeated in tick-tack-toe by a chicken. Not so. That was not the entire purpose of our walk. I won't deny that it happened, but it was not the entire purpose.

The purpose, I specifically told Fraser, was to give him a glimpse of downtown. I like to walk in big cities even more than I like to walk in small towns. In a relatively compact city like San Francisco, you can start at Fisherman's Wharf and spend the afternoon in a walk that takes in, among other attractions, the Italian district, Chinatown, the financial district, and the historic area that gave the world both beatniks and topless dancing. I even walk in Los Angeles — sometimes in Venice, where the funky beach reminds me a bit of what Santa Monica was like when I was a child. On Venice Beach, Alice and the girls and I once saw a man blowing truly spectacular soap bubbles the size of watermelons — still the symbol for me of the tendency of people in Southern California to become awfully good at something that isn't terribly important. When friends from out of town come to New York, I often suggest that we take a walk downtown, even if I harbor no plans to see them humiliated in a sporting contest.

The announcement that we were going to take a walk downtown brought to Fraser a look of what I'm afraid is characteristic befuddlement — although the mention of downtown might confuse even a person of normal alertness. In most American cities, what people mean by downtown is the central business district. One exception is New Orleans, where downtown means downriver from Canal Street and the central business district is called, of all things, the central business district. New York, of course, is an exception to any rule — except the old scientific truth that putting too many rats in a cage will cause them to snap at each other now and then. In New York, downtown never means the place where the department stores are — that's called midtown — and what it does mean can depend completely on who's talking about what.

To me, for instance, living downtown means living in Greenwich Village, the legend-encrusted old downtown neighborhood that will probably never amass enough respectable burghers and expensive restaurants and condo conversions to obliterate its lingering aura of bohemianism. (People in the Village traditionally take the notion of up and down town almost literally; it's still common to hear a dyed-in-the-wool Villager say, "Whenever I try to go above 14th Street, I get the bends.") To a New Yorker who is making his pile by fiddling with money, working downtown means working on Wall Street, an area that the typical Villager treats with disdain, of course, even if his forebears' efforts there were what enabled him to buy his Village brownstone. To some people who like to stay up until three or four in the morning and figure that you can't be too particular about the company you keep at that hour, going downtown means frequenting clubs in places like Tribeca — a definition of the word that was certainly not relevant for our purposes, I told Fraser, since he is much too old for such carryings-on.

All of that made Fraser look even more befuddled than usual, so I explained to him precisely the parts of downtown Manhattan we'd cover in our walk:

"Starting at my house, we'll walk down Bleecker Street in what's still a more or less Italian part of the Village, and then we'll cross Houston Street into the South Village, which is an Italian neighborhood, even though these days some of the Italians turn out to be Portuguese. That puts us right next to SoHo, where we'll stop in an art gallery or two to stuff a little culture down you. Then I'm afraid we have an awkward couple of blocks in what I suppose you'd call the machine tool district; we won't be jostled by a lot of other tourists there. Then Little Italy. Then we cross Canal Street into Chinatown for lunch. And then, if you've still got the courage for it, we head straight to the Chinatown Fair amusement arcade, where you can play tick-tack-toe against the smartest chicken you've ever seen in your entire life."

By maintaining a brisk pace — something we had no intention of doing — someone could cover all of that ground in half an hour. One of the reasons New York is such a terrific city for walking is the same reason that it's often so maddening: everything is jammed together. Another reason is that it's constantly changing. Fifteen years ago, what we now know as SoHo — the collection of art galleries and boutiques and restaurants and chic lofts that gets its name from being just South of Houston Street — was an industrial area whose lofts were occupied by hat makers and paper-box companies. Tribeca (Tri-angle Below Canal) is of even more recent trendifi-cation. At first glance, the South Village has the look of a long-established neighborhood. At Joe's Dairy, on Sullivan Street, women from the tenements that line Sullivan and Thompson and Macdougal were passing the time together when we stopped in to get some fresh mozzarella for the journey. Every June for as long as anyone can remember, the church across the street, St. Anthony, has presided over a feast that turns three or four blocks of Sulli-van into a fairway dominated by *calzone* and *zep-pole* and fried-sausage sandwiches. Still, even the South Village is a neighborhood that's changing. On a couple of blocks I pointed out to Fraser where the new next-door neighbor of an old-fashioned South Village pork store was a shop specializing in some-thing like art deco — an indication that the landlord would treat the pork store's next lease as an appro-priate time to make the blissful transition from South Village rents to SoHo rents, and another neigh-borhood shopkeeper would be ground into New York real estate sausage. Fraser just nodded. His mouth was full of mozzarella.

"I'm glad you're keeping your strength up," I told him. "This chicken you'll be going against is no pushover. In fact, I've never seen him defeated."

Fraser straightened his shoulders, and tried to assume an expression as confident and courageous as a man with his mouth full of freshly made mozzarella can assume — and we continued down Sullivan Street.

Yes, I tell the same stories to everyone I take on the tour. Let's face it, all of us tour guides tell the same stories again and again. Fraser didn't ask if he was getting canned commentary — either he wasn't interested or he didn't think of it — but if he had, I would have told him that at least my stories are true, more or less. I happen to live near a rather picturesque mews in the Village, and hardly a weekend passes without my hearing a tour guide tell a group of tourists some lie about its history. One guide regularly tells the tourists that Alfred Hitchcock shot *Rear Window* in the mews, even though it doesn't look remotely like the setting for *Rear Window*. In fact, as I pass the lighting cables and vintage cars and klieg lights that seem to be on my block constantly, it sometimes occurs to me that *Rear Window* may be the only Hollywood movie *not* shot in the Village. Somehow, though, the tourists in front of the mews are too passive or too polite to challenge these tales — which means, I suppose, that they're all out-of-towners. If there were New Yorkers on the tour, that line about *Rear Window* would start people in the crowd yelling, "Who's he kidding?" or "Give us a break, willya buddy?" or "Who's he think he's dealing with, a bunch of farmers?"

Anyway, the stories I told Fraser were old but true — even though he doesn't always give the impression of being someone who would know the difference. At Zito's, an Italian bakery on Bleecker Street, I pointed out the picture that Berenice Abbott, a distinguished American photographer, took of Zito's in the thirties — a picture that could have been taken yesterday except that the bread price shown is a nickel a loaf. In the twenties, when Zito's had one of the few decent ovens in the neighborhood, Italian housewives in nearby tenement houses would arrange to bake their bread there — they identified each of their loaves with a symbol in the dough — and I told Fraser that a friend of mine named Wally Popolizio, whose mother was among those housewives, seems to be a happier man because he knows that anytime he decides he might want a Popolizio coat of arms the bread symbol could serve as a central design element.

Walking past the galleries and boutiques and restaurants of West Broadway, SoHo's main drag, I told Fraser a few I-can-remember-when stories — the sort of stories that begin "I can remember when the first restaurant opened in SoHo . . ." or "I can remember when artists were able to afford lofts here even without moonlighting as investment bankers . . ." We also dropped into Dean & DeLuca, a breathtaking food store, just in case Fraser felt that he might be helped along his way by a white chocolate mousse tart or a few muscat raisins in brandy or some Pouligny St. Pierre ("No, you can't drink it, Fraser; it's cheese"). He was looking a bit peaked, I thought, and it occurred to me that what I had said about the chicken's being undefeated might have finally sunk in. Also, as promised, we went into one art gallery. We picked the O. K. Harris Gallery, on West Broadway, which I've usually found to be good for a surprise or two. When we emerged, Fraser didn't look as if he had gained any vitality, but, unless I miss my guess, he did appear just a tad more cultured.

There were no stories in the machine tool district. I simply don't know any machine tool stories, at least none that I thought would cheer up a man who seemed preoccupied by an impending encounter with a chicken. After a couple of blocks, though, we were in Little Italy, walking by the ornate pile that was formerly the police headquarters and, as such, was known to some in the neighborhood as St. John the Fuzz. A much larger Italian neighborhood than the South Village, Little Italy has always been a center of southern Italian restaurants. In fact, in what I have always thought of as the War of the Red and the White — the split between the traditional tomato sauce joints and the fancier cream sauce restaurants that claim some connection with places like Milan or Venice — Mulberry Street, one of the principal streets of Little Italy, is the nearly impregnable redoubt of the Red forces. I say nearly impregnable because at some point Georgine Carmella — a blatantly White restaurant with understated design and a menu that included such dishes as spinach risotto and roast quail — showed up on Mulberry Street, and managed to prosper for a number of years, like a daredevil commando unit operating behind enemy lines.

Even on the buildings whose ground floors have some of the best-known Red restaurants on Mulberry, I pointed out to Fraser, the business on the second floor is likely to be identified by Chinese letters. Chinatown used to be a small island in Little Italy. Since the mid-sixties, though, when the United States changed an immigration law that had permitted almost no legal immigration by Chinese, Chinatown in New York has grown at a pace that has chewed away at Little Italy and swallowed up some neighborhoods to the east and, eventually, created new Chinatowns in Brooklyn and Queens.

In recent years, I told Fraser as we edged past a market on Canal Street that displayed odd-looking vegetables and live crabs and fish that were still flopping around, there has been another change wrought by immigrants from Hong Kong. A lot of people from Hong Kong, unlike most immigrants to the United States, arrive with considerable cash and expensive tastes. Because of the Hong Kong immigrants' standards of comfort, some of the best restaurants in Chinatown these days have the sort of flash and amenities that ten years ago would have caused them to be dismissed by Chinatown denizens as "uptown Chinese." I explained all of that to Fraser as a way to warn him that we were about to have lunch at a restaurant called 20 Mott, which had credit cards, a beer license, a fancy glass façade, and, as it happens, first-rate dim sum.

Fraser said he liked the dim sum, but it seemed to me that he was a bit off his feed. To give him something to look forward to, I told him that anybody who beats the chicken in tick-tack-toe wins a large bag of fortune cookies that must be worth thirty-five or forty cents, only slightly less than it costs to play the game. By the time we finished lunch, Fraser seemed to have his old competitive spirit back.

It flagged, though, when we arrived at the amusement arcade just down Mott Street and Fraser inspected the playing field. There was the chicken, pecking away behind glass in a large case that had a scoreboard to show the progress of the contest and letters that lit up to say "YOUR TURN" or "BIRD'S TURN."

The scoreboard also contained buttons that Fraser could use to indicate his X's and O's; the chicken did that by pecking at a board that was in a private area of his cage behind some opaque glass.

"But he gets to go first!" Fraser said after he dropped in his fifty cents and the contest got under way. "That's a great advantage."

"But you're a human being, and he's just a chicken," I pointed out. "Surely there should be some advantage in that."

Maybe not. Fraser lost. He demanded another game. He lost again. Finally he played the chicken to a draw — a performance that does not qualify for the fortune cookies. As we walked through the cacophony of video games into Mott Street, Fraser looked disconsolate. He mumbled something about its all being quite embarrassing.

"Don't worry," I said. "I'll never tell a soul. You can count on me."

# 11

## A Woman's Place

I SUPPOSE YOU COULD SAY that we went to Guadeloupe one cold winter as a gesture of support for its efforts to celebrate female chefs. Sure, I figured on polishing off a good number of stuffed crabs while I was in the area and Sarah intended to put into effect an intricately constructed tan plan, but that was all part of the celebration.

Guadeloupe happens to be an island that has as its major annual event every August a *fête des cuisinières* at which several dozen women chefs put together a five-hour banquet of Creole specialties after having visited the cathedral to ask the blessing of Saint Laurent, patron saint of cooks. I can't see going to the Caribbean in August even for a five-hour Creole banquet, but the mere existence of the *fête des cuisinières* as the most important event of the year was an indication that these people had their priorities in order. It's the sort of thing that can make you wonder why vacationers spend so much time in places where the major annual event is a horse race or the opening of Parliament. It's certainly the sort of thing that made me wonder why so much of my time in the Caribbean had been spent in former British colonies where the chefs seemed to have been looked after by Saint Nigel, the Anglican saint of gray meat and veggies.

I am, after all, someone who celebrated female chefs even during the early years of the women's movement, when reaction against the old saw about a woman's place being in the kitchen was so strong that feminist friends attacked me for my public effort to get Mrs. Lisa Mosca of Mosca's restaurant in Waggaman, Louisiana, the Nobel Prize for the perfection of her baked oysters. It was during those years that my friend William Edgett Smith, the man with the Naugahyde palate, proudly took us to a restaurant run by some sort of radical feminist collective — this place had a name something like Juno's Revenge — and seemed stunned when I informed him, halfway through the main course, that the restaurant had obviously been founded to eradicate the false notion that women can by nature cook.

The extremes of that period eventually became no more than historical footnotes — although even now, when there's a sudden shift in the weather, I can still taste the burnt crust of Juno's truly horrifying chicken potpie. In Guadeloupe, it seemed perfectly natural for me to be sitting at Chez Violetta and admiring the awards and honors that the proprietress displayed on the walls. The proprietress, Violetta Saint-Phor, happened to be that year's president of the organization of women chefs known as L'Association Mutualiste des Cuisinières. A group picture taken of the association at the annual festival was among the decorations on the wall, along with a huge color picture of Violetta Saint-Phor herself, dressed in the bright print dress and madras headdress traditional among the women chefs of Guadeloupe. As I looked around, it occurred to me that eating at Chez Violetta was something like eating at one of those restaurants that display the name and trophies of some hero like Stan Musial or Mickey Mantle. But that was before I tasted the *matété de crabes* — a dish that might be described as a sort of crab stew, in the sense that a particularly stunning bouillabaisse served on the Marseille docks might be described as a sort of fish soup. Once I had tasted the *matété de crabes*, I was reminded of a significant difference between the celebrity of Violetta Saint-Phor and the celebrity of someone like Stan Musial: Violetta Saint-Phor did not become renowned for runs batted in.

Sitting there at Chez Violetta with Alice and Abigail and Sarah, finishing up the *matété de crabes* with the serving spoon, I suppose I felt that I had finally come to a place where women chefs were given the recognition they deserve. I don't speak only of my attempt to get the Nobel Prize for Mrs. Mosca — an unsuccessful attempt, as it turned out, since they gave it to Kissinger that year. Despite having my efforts completely ignored by the city officials of Kansas City, I struggled for years to have a major Missouri River bridge named in memory of Chicken Betty Lucas, the legendary pan-frier of midwestern poultry. I was the tourist who years before in Martinique had spent much of his beach time composing a poem for the brilliant Mrs. Palladino ("I left no smidgen / Of your pigeon"). It was I who mentioned the possibility of building a statue on Fifth Avenue of Edna Lewis's corn bread, brushing aside those who said that corn bread made out of granite was bound to look dry. I had been active.

I knew that some people thought I might have been avoiding Guadeloupe because it is officially a part of France. Not so. I wouldn't deny that over the years, despite those pleasant stays in Provence and my absolute passion for *taureaux piscine*, I might have had an unkind word or two to say about France when the subject being discussed was relative levels of courtesy (low) or bureaucracy (high). But I have forgiven the French a lot, usually at mealtime. Also, it wasn't clear precisely how French Guadeloupe is. It's true that even the line for passport control was triangular — the shape so ingrained among the French that I had expected to see it even at the Champs-Élysées Burger King, *Maison du Whopper* — but when we reached the immigration officer I found that he did not have a scratchy pen and did not say, "Granmuzzer's maiden name?"

People who live in Guadeloupe — I suppose they could be called Guadeloupais, although I like the sound of Guadeloupeans — do speak French, of course, but not in a way that makes them terribly concerned with the imperfections of a visitor's pronunciation. They don't seem to care much about your granmuzzer's maiden name, either. Although Guadeloupe is closely connected with metropolitan France in any number of ways, it's more than four thousand miles from Paris; obviously only a limited number of its residents can afford to go to the elite universities there for the postgraduate course in essential rudeness. On the other hand, everyone seemed to be able to do flawless French fries. As we were digging into the *pommes frites* we bought one day from an outdoor stand in Gosier, a little town near the line of beach hotels just east of Pointe-à-Pitre, I had to acknowledge that there was a certain nobility in the French having spread the French-frying skill around the world when the English were spending a lot of time and energy trying to plant the notion of parliamentary democracy.

The true French contribution to eating in Guadeloupe, of course, is not French food, although we had some French food good enough to put me in a mood to let bygones be bygones. Simply the presence of flawless *pommes frites* right there in Gosier, for instance, was almost enough to make me forgive the bank clerk in Lyon who insisted that twelve forms (seven of them in triplicate) had to be filled out in order to change fifty dollars American into francs. The young Frenchman in charge of an elegant little restaurant in Pointe-à-Pitre called La Canne à Sucre managed with one dish — an appetizer listed as *pain de poisson* — to make me feel a bit guilty about having given some particularly unpleasant Paris shopkeepers the impression that I was going to have them rubbed out by a mob enforcer from Chicago.

In Guadeloupe and Martinique, the best thing the French did for eating was to contribute their culinary approach as one of the elements — African cooking and Caribbean ingredients were among the others — that went into the evolution of Creole cuisine, the sort of food that made Musial-size heroines of the members of L'Association Mutualiste des Cuisinières. I don't mean that I wasn't grateful to find on Guadeloupe cooks from other parts of the French-frying world. At a restaurant that came about because somebody from what had been French Vietnam married someone from what is still French Réunion, an island in the Indian Ocean, we had a meal that was enhanced for me by the knowledge that it almost certainly made me the first person from my high school in Kansas City ever to have eaten Réunionnaise food.

Still, I hadn't come to Guadeloupe for a gastronomic tour of what we used to call the French sphere of influence. I had come to eat *crabes farcis* (stuffed crabs), *blaff* (the only onomatopoeic stew I know about), *colombo de lambi* (conch curry), and *acras à morue* (codfish fritters). I had come armed with a book I had purchased in Martinique ten years before: *The French West-Indies Through Their Cookery* by Dr. André Nègre. In that book, the good doctor quickly dismissed French cuisine by saying, "Many Frenchmen from the Métropole come to these countries, so new to them, with the settled idea that steak-and-chips and roast chicken are the summit of cookery." I was aware that Dr. Nègre had even harsher words for American cooking: "One can reach gastronomy only at the last stage of refinement and culture. This is why the U.S., which has not had two centuries of existence yet and which knows no ancient culture, has no proper cookery, except the very

French one of a few hundred head cooks from our country, whom the Yankees have imported in order to be delighted by those masters."

I remembered having been a little irritated by that remark ten years before. I remembered having thought that anyone who is under the impression that an ancient culture guarantees a great cuisine has never tasted Navajo fry-bread. Still, I did pack Dr. Nègre's book, along with a lot of restaurant tips, when we headed for Guadeloupe. As the French have discovered, I'm not one to hold a grudge.

I knew precisely what Dr. Nègre meant about people who believe grilled chicken and French fries are the summit of cookery. Alice and I happened to be in Guadeloupe with two of them — Abigail and Sarah, both of whom might have been flattered to learn that their eating habits marked them as people from the Métropole. Grilled chicken and French fries were what they were eating one afternoon when it occurred to me that I might have shirked my duties toward inspiring them with some of the more exotic triumphs of the women cooks of Guadeloupe — women who, in Dr. Nègre's words, "possess the art of carelessly throwing at a glance, and without any previous dosage, the exact quantity of pimento and of chives necessary for the stuffing of a sucking pig." I had once had a more evangelical feeling about these matters — more like Dr. Nègre's — but then my daughters passed the age where they might respond to an unknown dish simply by closing their mouths and shaking their heads vigorously. They advanced to the age at which they could, if so inclined, respond by saying something like "Daddy, I hope you're not going to make a scene about how absolutely fascinating it would be to eat bat stew."

A few years before, I might have tried to trade off a few strange foodstuffs for exemption from the broadening cultural experiences that are supposedly a traveling parent's responsibility, even in the Caribbean: "If you try one bite of *gratinée de christophines*, I promise not to describe the meteorological phenomenon of the rain forest, take you on an architectural tour of Pointe-à-Pitre, or discuss the topographical differences between Guadeloupe's two land masses, the flat Grande-Terre and the mountainous Basse-Terre." But they were too old to fall for that sort of thing; they were perfectly aware that I knew nothing at all about the meteorological phenomenon of the rain forest. I figured I'd settle for the fact that they had at least taken to eating *acras à morue* and had survived at least one broadening cultural experience. It took place in a shorefront restaurant on Basse-Terre. Through either a misunderstanding or some unannounced changes in the kitchen, a waiter had brought them curry of goat rather than curry of chicken — a switch they had been unaware of until the waiter slowed up at our table late in the meal and said, "Bah, bah."

As it happened, while they were eating grilled chicken and French fries, I was eating *boudin de lambi*, conch sausage. This was at what amounted to a beach canteen, the sort of place that on a North American beach might be expected to stretch its repertoire no further than cheeseburgers. It was on the beach of what had once been the Hôtel Les Alizés, near a charming town on the Atlantic side of Grande-Terre called Le Moule. The *boudin de lambi* was excellent. So were the French fries. "This is an island where you can get conch sausage at a beach canteen," I informed my daughters. "What else is there to say?"

One day we went by boat to Terre-de-Haut, the main island of Les Saintes, a cluster of tiny islands seven miles off the tip of Guadeloupe. Terre-de-Haut has its charms — terrific beaches, a picturesque village filled with gingerbread bungalows — but it's not the sort of place where a traveler would expect a great variety of foodstuffs. It's remote. Virtually nothing is grown on it. Its natural supply of fresh water never varies: none. As we disembarked, children came to peddle a delicious coconut pastry that's a specialty of the island, and for lunch we ate another specialty, smoked fish. All of that was fine. But what truly impressed me was the menu of a

simple restaurant called Chez Janine, which we
passed on the harbor as we were walking back to
the boat. It listed codfish fritters, stuffed crab, beignets of *aubergine*, Creole sausage, crudités, tomato
salad, goat curry, chicken curry, court bouillon of
fish, fricassee of conch, fricassee of octopus, ragout
of goat, grilled fish, grilled chicken, pork chops,
*aubergine* au gratin, *christophine* au gratin, papayas
au gratin, purée of breadfruit, two kinds of rice, banana flambé, coconut flan, and banana beignets. At
the side of a building there was a sign that announced the availability of take-out French fries.

On Guadeloupe itself, of course, that sort of variety was commonplace. I would get up in the morning and read out loud a list of the restaurant pro-
prietresses, just to let myself know the possibilities
of the day: "Prudence Marcelin of Chez Prudence–
Folie Plage, Félicité Doloir of Le Barbaroc, Lucienne
Salcède of Le Karocoli, Jeanne Carmelite of La Ré-
serve . . ." There were times, of course, when a
meal persuaded me that the name of that chef
would have to be dropped at my next morning's
reading — a restaurant in Guadeloupe that gets accustomed to producing stuffed crab for busloads of
French tourists is, sooner or later, as routine as a
restaurant on Cape Cod that grows accustomed to
shoveling out clam chowder for busloads of American tourists — but then we would eat at a place like

Chez Clara, in the little Basse-Terre town of Sainte-Rose. Chez Clara turned out to be on the porch of an old house across the street from the shore — a porch with a tin roof, heavy beams, and a Martini blackboard that listed the specialties. It was run by Clara Lesueur, who had worked as a fashion model in Paris for a while, although not long enough to get sullen. Its specialties, we learned, were curried skate, grilled lobster, and stuffed crab. By dessert I was feeling so magnanimous that I had decided to restore some names that had been stricken from my morning reading of women chefs; I had decided that whoever had served us something that seemed uninspired was probably saving her best shot for the *fête des cuisinières* in August. I also decided to compose a poem to Clara Lesueur: "I long to roost / Near your *langouste*."

# 12

# Abigail y Yo

I SUPPOSE YOU COULD SAY that Abigail was living out my fantasies, if you were the sort of person who liked to rub it in. Abigail had decided to spend the semester studying in Madrid. In long letters and Sunday telephone calls, she filled us in on her life in Spain: sunny afternoons at the boat pond in El Retiro Gardens, a weekend spent at the annual fiesta of a tiny village in Galicia, long discussions in the dormitory of a Spanish friend she had met in the subway and sometimes referred to as *la amiga del Metro*.

"It sounds absolutely terrific," Alice said one Sunday on the telephone, just after Abigail had told us how exciting it was to be able to understand lectures in Spanish.

There was a moment's pause in the conversation — a pause that I, in playing the role fathers have traditionally played in expensive long-distance conversations with college-aged children, might have been expected to fill with "Well, O.K. Fine. Goodbye." Instead, I said, "I'd like to tell you how I feel about all of this, Abigail, but I don't know the Spanish word for 'envy.'"

I might have known that word. I might have known a lot of Spanish words. When I was in Spain just after college, I had the opportunity to remain in Madrid for a year to study, and I didn't take it — a decision I think about often, in the way a businessman might reflect on his decision to pass up that patch of scrubland that is now occupied by the third-largest-grossing shopping center west of the Mississippi.

I was serious about Spanish. I was never serious about French. Sure, I still exchange nasty remarks with a Paris taxi driver now and again. But my public announcement that, more or less as a matter of policy, I do not use verbs in French was widely taken as an acknowledgment that I could no longer be considered a diligent student of the language. I never made a systematic attempt at Italian, and I have simply ignored German. Spanish is my foreign language.

More to the point, Spanish is not my foreign language. In my good moments, I've been able to say what I needed to say in Spanish, although not in a way that was likely to attract compliments on my grammar and syntax. In my bad moments, my attempts to speak Spanish have a lot in common with my attempts to speak Italian, which is to say that they lean heavily on gestures. I have always had trouble understanding Spanish; there have been times when a paragraph of Spanish has sounded to me like one long word.

Even when I seem to be doing pretty well in Spanish, I can run out of it, the way someone might run out of flour or eggs. A few years after I passed up the chance to stay in Madrid, some friends and I went to Baja California to mark an occasion I can no longer remember, and I became the group's spokesman to the owner of our motel, a Mrs. Gonzales, who spoke no English. Toward the end of a very long evening, as I listened to her complain about some excess of celebration on our part, I suddenly realized that I had run out of Spanish. It wasn't merely that I couldn't think of the Spanish words for what I wanted to say ("I am mortified, Mrs. Gonzales, to learn that someone in our group might have behaved in a manner so inappropriate, not to say disgusting"). I couldn't think of any Spanish words at all. Desperately rummaging around in the small bin of Spanish in my mind, I could come up with nothing but the title of a Calderón play I had once read, to no lasting effect, in a Spanish literature course.

"Mrs. Gonzales," I said. "Life is a dream."

She looked impressed and, I must say, surprised. She told me that I had said something really quite profound. I shrugged. It seemed the appropriately modest response; even if it hadn't been, it would have been all I could do until I managed to borrow a cup of Spanish from a neighbor. Eventually I came to look back on the experience as just about the only time I was truly impressive in a foreign language.

Every few years I work up the energy to hurl myself again at the Spanish language, in the hope of making the breakthrough that people who learn foreign languages are always talking about. The evidence of my failures clutters my house — the Spanish-language tapes jammed in the back of a drawer, the absolutely guaranteed three-volume teach-yourself-Spanish course that falls from the highest shelf in the closet as I fumble for a suitcase I thought I might have stashed up there some years before. It has often occurred to me that I'll never speak Spanish. People who spend a lot of time around newspapers are afflicted with the ability to imagine what's sometimes called the drop-head of their obituary — an obituary large enough to call for a drop-head as well as the main headline has traditionally been the principal side-benefit of the trade — and the drop-head I have sometimes imagined for myself is "Monolingual Reporter Succumbs."

Sometimes, though, I think my Spanish break-through is somewhere on the next cassette. When I decided to visit Abigail in Spain, I decided at the same time to give Spanish one more try. For a few weeks I spent an hour a day speaking Spanish with a young woman from Spain who was teaching at New York University. In Spanish, I told her a lot of things about America — how the wheat got to Kansas in the last century, for instance, which is probably something that nobody in her town in Spain mentions often — and she told me that I did not appear to know the difference between *por* and *para*. I think I learned a lot about Spanish from her, although I continue to believe that no one truly understands the difference between *por* and *para*. I bought a new Spanish dictionary. I also bought one of those pocket computers that translate from Spanish to English and back again. On the plane to Madrid, I was carrying my Spanish–English dictionary, my translating computer, a copy of *The Old Gringo* in English and of *Gringo Viejo* in Spanish, an issue of a Madrid newspaper called *El Pais*, and a volume that I would have to name if I happened to be among those asked by some literary journal to list their favorite books of the year, *301 Spanish Verbs*. In the interest of moderation, I had passed up *501 Spanish Verbs*, by the same author, but I felt overequipped anyway — like some Wall Street hobbyist who, upon deciding he might like to do some biking around the city, immediately buys a fourteen-hundred-dollar Italian racing bike, a pair of imported leather biking gloves, three kinds of pumps, and the sort of clothing that might be seen on a competitor in the Tour de France. I was prepared. When I arrived in Spain to visit Abigail, I intended to speak Spanish. I intended to understand Spanish. I had a fallback position, of course: Abigail speaks very good English.

"Just give me a little hint of what it's about," I said to Ginny. Abigail and I and Ginny, a fellow student of Abigail's at the Instituto Internacional, were in a *tapas* bar off the Plaza Mayor, eating a sort of seafood salad and a pile of tiny fried fish. We were discussing a Cervantes play called *El Retablo de las Maravillas*, which Ginny and some other American students were going to put on at the Instituto the following week. By having Ginny give me some idea of the plot, I was hoping to avoid getting off on the wrong foot when I saw the actual performance. What I dreaded was finding myself, just before the final curtain, suddenly disabused of the notion that I had been watching a play about the early days of major-league baseball.

Abigail didn't seem concerned about being able to understand the play. Basically, Abigail could understand Spanish. It hadn't come in any blinding flash, she said. At some point she simply realized that she had been taking in what was said by the contestants on a television game show that the family she lived with watched every Monday night — *El Precio Justo*, a two-hour Spanish version of *The Price Is Right*.

My record in attempting to understand Spanish theatrical works was not encouraging. As far as I could remember, the last time I had sat in the audience of a Spanish production, game but bewildered, was in Vermont, where many years ago I spent several weeks in the summer Spanish program at Middlebury College. The Middlebury summer language programs are widely esteemed in the field; I must be one of their rare failure stories. The summer I was there, Middlebury had half a dozen programs, each of them using a language not simply as the language of instruction but as the language students were expected to speak in the dining hall and the dormitories and on the playing fields. The students were virtually all Americans, many of them high school language teachers working on their master's degrees, but within days most of them had fallen into the stereotypes then identified with the countries whose languages they were studying. It was common to refer to those studying French, say, as "the French" — and to take it for granted that they would spend a lot of time criticizing one another's accents. "The Russians" were stiff-necked and just about impossible to deal with when it came to assigning hours and tables at a shared dining hall. If a great horde of people, all of them looking perfectly capable of singing loud drinking songs, burst into the local tavern together, one of the regulars was bound to mutter, in English, "Jesus, it's the Germans." I can't actually remember what "the Spanish" were noted for, but if my own experience is any guide, I'm afraid it might have been indolence.

This time, though, I was serious, which was why I wanted Ginny to give me a little head start on *El Retablo de las Maravillas*. She seemed willing enough. "It's about some gypsies who come to a village and scare the villagers," she told me. "The villagers are kind of conformists, and the gypsies say, for instance, that all smart people can see rats on this screen. So all the villagers say they can see rats."

Ginny fell silent, and began poking around the seafood salad for one of the less suspicious-looking creatures.

"That's it?" I asked.

"Well, I don't want to give away the whole plot," she said.

I was somewhat comforted by the knowledge that when I saw *El Retablo de las Maravillas* I'd

have more stage Spanish under my belt. Abigail and
I had decided to spend the weekend in Barcelona,
and a young friend of ours who was living there,
Anya Schiffrin, had promised to take us around to
some of her favorite attractions — none of which, I
suspect, would have made a list compiled by the
Bureau of Tourism. I knew that on Anya's tour we'd
be seeing the show at an old music hall and at the
sort of nightclub where the entertainment is provided by the waitresses and the barman and, now
and then, an inspired amateur from among the evening's clientele.

By the time we took our seats that Friday night at
the music hall, a place called El Molino, I was feeling that the first two days of my latest attempt at
speaking Spanish had gone pretty well. In both
Madrid and Barcelona, I had used only Spanish at
the hotel — I knew that just about everyone involved spoke English, but I pretended that I was at
Middlebury — and I hadn't ended up in the broom
closet. I had chatted fairly easily, if briefly, with
some of the vendors at La Bouquería, Barcelona's
stupendous public market, where Abigail and I had
exhausted our Spanish adjectives expressing appreciation of a sandwich made by rubbing tomatoes on
the inside of a toasted baguette and then loading it
up with fresh anchovies. The unfortunate episode
at lunch — when I spoke to the waiter, he replied

to Anya — was something I had decided to accept as a small and temporary setback.

El Molino turned out to be an appropriately rococo vaudeville house with two tiers of ornate boxes overlooking the orchestra seats. The entire place was painted red — what seemed to be dozens of coats, resulting in the sort of shiny finish that certain expensive decorators put on the dining room walls of rich people in Manhattan. Although the audience sat in conventional rows of theater seats, drinks were served, and the price of admission was folded into the price of the first drink. To accommodate the drinks, there was a narrow counter running along the backs of the seats in front of you — a menace as well as a convenience, Anya warned us, because if the man in front of you absent-mindedly put his arm around his wife's shoulders he'd be very likely to put your beer right in your lap.

The show at El Molino featured chorus girls wearing a staggering array of costumes that I would describe, in general, as having too many feathers in some places and not enough in others. There were also chorus boys, although that term probably reflects insufficient respect for their age. Most of the production numbers had people in feathers moving in unison on the stage — dancing in the sense that Rex Harrison in *My Fair Lady* was singing. During feather changes, pairs of comics came out to do sketches that required nearly constant leering. The themes of the production numbers were established by ever-changing backdrops. Anya apparently noticed a puzzled look on my face when, in front of a backdrop that was difficult to identify except for a street sign that said VIA VENETO, a woman sang a song to a man while being accompanied, more or less, by eight or ten chorus girls who were dressed in something suggesting Latin American peasant women — although I can't say I've ever actually seen a Latin American peasant woman wearing a rug on her head. "Every day, she's heard a voice of a man and she fell in love with him through the voice and that's him," Anya whispered. "Why the costumes, I don't know."

The audience at El Molino — certainly including our party — was enthusiastic, but I wouldn't claim that I actually followed what was being said on stage. I had the same problem the next night at the Bodega Bohemia, where the only entertainer who didn't carry drinks or wipe down the bar during the other acts was the piano player, a gray-haired old gentleman in a business suit who looked like a retired high school principal returning to accompany the senior boys choir, just to keep his hand in. In both places, some people spoke rapidly and used a lot of slang and double-entendres. I explained to Anya that I was working, at best, with single-entendre Spanish.

Anya told us that it had taken her two or three trips to catch on to the patter at El Molino herself. Abigail reminded me that in Barcelona I had enjoyed a triumph or two in comprehending ordinary, nonleering Spanish. At lunch one day at a little seafood place in Barceloneta, the dock area, the proprietress, a jolly friend of Anya's I'll call Raquel, had told us why she avoids trips on boats or airplanes: she believes an accident could easily put her in the water, she can't swim, and she therefore assumes that she would be eaten by sharks. As I was telling Abigail that Raquel's precautions sounded sensible enough to me, I realized that Raquel had been speaking Spanish.

I didn't feel that my Spanish had been tested on some of our stops. That had certainly been true at the dance hall Anya took us to after Bodega Bohemia — a vast place where a number of the most lavishly dressed ballroom dancers seemed to get along just as well without partners. At the event we attended on Sunday, a Sevillana festival at the Barcelona bullring, I don't think anyone could have made out all of the lyrics blaring from the huge loudspeakers on the stage. In the ring, thousands of Andalusians, most of them people who had come to Catalonia for factory jobs, danced and sang and waved green-and-white Andalusian flags for seven or eight hours. Some of the participants were in the sort of clothing Americans associate with flamenco dancers, but some of them had got into costume by wearing green jackets or green hats; looking out on the crowd, I sometimes had to shake off the impression that I had come across a horde of Boston Irish who had been taken suddenly and implausibly with a passion for melodramatic dancing.

When we drove from the Sevillana festival to our final meal in Barcelona, I told Anya how much we had enjoyed the tour.

"Oh no!" she said. "I forgot to take you to the museum of the dead, where they let you sit in the hearses."

"Not to worry," I said. "It's always nice to save one treat for the next visit."

I understood the taxi driver who drove us in from the Madrid airport when we returned from Barcelona. We talked about Americans and Russians. He said that Americans were more open than Russians. I thought about telling him how the Russians had behaved when they had to share the dining hall at Middlebury, even though I was quite aware that those Russians were not real Russians. When you're uncertain in a language, there's a temptation to use what you've got. The taxi driver told me not to worry about not understanding the comics at El Molino;

he said Catalans didn't talk right. The taxi driver spoke excellent Spanish himself. It occurred to me that if I were put in charge of the government broadcasting system in Spain, the first two announcers I'd try to hire would be the taxi driver and Raquel. She might even be willing to come to Madrid for the broadcasts, since you don't have to fly over any water to get there from Barcelona.

The conversations with Raquel and the taxi driver had been brief, of course. The real test was whether I could understand a lecture given by one of Abigail's professors. Abigail told me that the lecture in her politics class would be about the period in the late fifties when Franco's regime gradually began to change — a period that happened to coincide with my first visit to Spain. She was, I later realized, giving me a little head start. In class the next morning, I sat next to Abigail. I thought I was ready. I had spent some of the previous evening thumbing through *301 Spanish Verbs*. The professor began. He spoke beautifully clear Spanish, better even than the taxi driver's. He talked about the technocrats coming into government and about the role of Opus Dei and about the mystery that persists as to why Franco permitted the sort of economic development that he must have known would lead to an expanded middle class and demands for more freedom. I took notes.

"I understood everything," I said to Abigail at the end of the lecture.

Abigail said she was proud of me. "I knew you could do it," she said. "Maybe you ought to come to my history class tomorrow. You could be on a roll."

I understood history, too. I was gaining confidence. I did pretty well in conversation with Abigail's *amiga del Metro* and at dinner with the family Abigail was living with. I was beginning to think that if I were staying on until the next Monday I might be ready for a crack at *El Precio Justo*. The dramatic piece at hand, though, was not *El Precio Justo* but *El Retablo de las Maravillas*. On the night before I was due to leave Spain, we took our seats in the Instituto's auditorium for the performance.

I couldn't understand it. I couldn't understand it at all. For one awful moment I was convinced that it was being done in a language other than Spanish. When it was over, all I knew about it was that some gypsies came to a village where the peasants were rather conformist and told the peasants that smart people would be able to see the rats on a screen.

"What was that about?" I said to Abigail at the end of the play.

"I don't know," Abigail said. "I couldn't understand it."

At first I thought Abigail was just trying to make

me feel better, but then it turned out that her friends hadn't understood it either. Later in the evening I talked to Abigail's history teacher, a native of Mallorca who had appeared in the same play in high school, and she said she'd had some trouble understanding the play herself. That did make me feel better, although I was pretty sure that the history teacher had never been in doubt as to what language was being spoken.

The history teacher and I were speaking Spanish, of course. I decided that *El Retablo de las Maravillas* had been a special case. So was El Molino. Of course, you could argue that a lecture at the Instituto Internacional in politics or history would also amount to a special case — if you were that sort of person. The professor, after all, has organized the material systematically, and is accustomed to speaking to foreigners, and is dealing with a subject rich in cognates. That's not the way I look at it. When I think of those lectures what I remember is an encounter I had with a couple of American students after Abigail's history class. Abigail had suggested that I not accompany her to her history of art lecture ("Don't press your luck"), and I was on my way to the Metro.

"You're Abigail's father, aren't you?" one of the students said.

"We saw you in history," the other one explained.

"We thought you must be really bored sitting there, unless . . . do you understand Spanish?"

I hesitated for only a moment. "Yes," I said. "Yes, I do."

# 13

## Gelati Fever

I'VE ALWAYS THOUGHT that when a family travels abroad its members settle into identifiable roles, so that someone who truly knows, say, those four Americans who are chatting at an outdoor café in Florence could point to each of them in turn and say, "She explains the frescoes, she speaks a little Italian, she buys shoes, and he schleps the luggage."

I realize that people who think they truly know our family would point to me and say, "He looks for things to eat" or "He eats a somewhat embarrassing amount of Italian food, heavy on the tomato sauce." I have that reputation. It comes, I'm sure, partly from what Alice has said about my behavior the first time we traveled in Italy together, in 1965. According to the version of the story Alice has always told, I spent the drives between cities closely examining the Michelin guide to Italy, occasionally looking up from my research to say something like "If we take a left at the next town, we can swing by a promising-looking seafood joint, and I figure it's only about sixty kilometers out of the way."

As it happens, the version of the story Alice has always told is correct. But as Alice and I and Sarah prepared to spend a few weeks in Italy one summer, I had reason to believe that this trip would be different — and not simply because I had decided, on the advice of some serious eaters, to replace Michelin as my principal guide to the wonders of Italy with a book called *I Ristoranti di Veronelli*. (The tipsters said that the author, Luigi Veronelli, was so authoritative that I need not concern myself with the fact that he writes in Italian.) I had reason to believe that the roles we often assume when traveling in Europe might be adjusted. The reason was *gelato,* Italian ice cream.

I had heard that since our previous trip to Italy, a couple of years before, *gelaterias* had proliferated faster than Visa and MasterCard signs. It happens that I have always been able to pass up *gelato* or any other sort of dessert in Italy — perhaps because it has normally been offered just after I ate a somewhat embarrassing amount of Italian food. Although Sarah had the interest in ice cream usually associated with the teenage years — she was a specialist in chocolate chip and in the sort of ice cream novelty I had sometimes heard her describe after a bite or two as "weird but good" — I had occasionally seen her pass an ice cream outlet without slowing her pace. On previous trips to Italy, I had never seen Alice pass a *gelati* stand without stopping for at least an inspection — an inventory to ascertain the range of flavors, a check to see whether or not the color of the *nocciola* indicated pure hazelnuts, a perusal of the chocolate-and-nut mixtures like *giandula* and *baci*. During our stay in Taormina, I had noticed that a complete inspection was requiring a sample earlier and earlier in the day — until one morning I heard myself saying, in the unfamiliar tones of someone trying to exert a moderating influence, "Isn't it a bit soon after breakfast?" With the proliferation of *gelati* outlets, it occurred to me, the inspections and samplings could grow to the point at which an interpreter of roles could point to Alice and say, "She eats ice cream" — no matter how many frescoes she had explained.

In Venice, where we stopped for a few days because Sarah had always wanted to see the canals, it occurred to me that Italians who observed Alice entering a *gelateria* might take her for a person of official or even noble rank — and not simply because of my habit of calling her *principessa* when we're in

Italy. Whenever Alice swept into a *gelateria* in Venice, Sarah and I tended to be one or two steps behind, like a couple of second lieutenants who had been assigned as aides-de-camp. Sarah would be glancing around to see if the place just happened to carry some Italianate version of a Creamsicle. I would be holding a copy of Veronelli's guide, which I had bought within minutes of our arrival and which I spent any spare moment trying to make out. I couldn't seem to master his rating system, which consisted of awarding "*berrettoni, bottiglie, stella, alambicci e bichieri*" — unless that was the address of his publisher.

Italian ice cream purveyors always seem ready for an unannounced inspection. Ten or fifteen or twenty flavors are lined up in open stainless steel tanks, so that the color and a hint of the texture are apparent with a simple glance. Sometimes the fruit flavors are displayed with the real article on top — fresh strawberries on top of the strawberry ice cream, pears on top of the pear — just in case anybody has even a fleeting doubt about the authenticity of the ingredients. Next to the ice cream case there is likely to be a sign that says PRODUZIONE PROPRIA — homemade. The necessity of sampling a range of tastes for proper inspection is assumed. Someone dipping ice cream in Italy never acts surprised if a customer picks out a medium-size cone or cup and then selects five flavors to have stuffed into it.

The most magnificent display, though, could appear to wither as Alice made her way slowly down the rows of flavors. "The *crema* has that odd artificial color," she might say, or "The *giandula* doesn't look dark enough," or, most devastating of all, "It looks as if it came in manufactured blocks." A taste test could be even more exacting. The most serious one in Venice came at the Caffè Florian, on the Piazza San Marco, where one of Alice's ice cream touts had said that the *tartufo* might be worthy of her attention. A *tartufo* is a scoop of rich chocolate ice cream with a cherry in the middle and a crust of dark chocolate on the outside. Eating *tartufi* is a sort of sideline of Alice's, although she has always treated the cherry in the middle as something that wandered in by mistake. Alice was thinking that Florian's *tartufo* might salvage for Venice what had been a disappointing ice cream performance, marred by a limitation of flavors and the aftertaste of chemical ingredients. I think Alice was beginning to lean toward the theory, widespread among *gelati* fanciers, that in Italy ice cream flavors, like blood feuds, get richer and more satisfying as you move south.

I had been having problems of my own with *I Ristoranti di Veronelli*. I still couldn't seem to make out the rating system, although dinner at a seafood place called Trattoria La Corte Sconta, which had been awarded a mysterious symbol that looked like the ace of clubs, had led me to believe that any sort of notice by Veronelli might be enough of a recommendation for me. The rating system seemed to consist partly of awarding restaurants up to four tiny chef's toques, but there were also symbols like the ace of clubs and a heart. At first I had assumed that a heart next to a restaurant meant that it had a romantic ambience — I planned to avoid those, of course, on the proven theory that the proprietor of a romantic restaurant is probably spending too much of his time tending the fresh flowers and soothing the feelings of the strolling violinist and not enough of his time hectoring the chef — but after a rereading, if that's the word, I decided that a heart might indicate a restaurant that Veronelli couldn't measure in a conventional way because it was too close to his heart. I had thought Sarah might be able to lend a hand at translating — she had just completed her second and final year of Latin — but Sarah informed me that she had decided not to have anything more to do with Latin for the rest of her life, even in a good cause.

The Florian seemed to be an appropriate setting for a serious ice cream tasting. Inside, it had velvet settees and a mosaic floor and a bar of burnished wood. Its menu included, in four languages, a few paragraphs on its history: since 1720, it has been a gathering place for distinguished folks like the heroes of Venetian independence and Lord Byron and Charles Dickens and Marcel Proust. Its outdoor café had white wicker chairs with the Martini & Rossi logo on their backs. Its own orchestra was playing for the entertainment of its customers — proper waltzes, not "Hold That Tiger," which I had caught a café orchestra around the corner playing one afternoon. The Florian waiters were impeccable in wing collars, white bow ties, and white jackets with braided epaulets. One of them set a *tartufo* in front of Alice.

She picked up her spoon and took a small bite. Then she paused. Then she said, "I think that this *tartufo* is not successful."

I looked over at the waiter. Had he heard? I could imagine the scene if he had:

Suddenly he looks dejected. This is a man who only moments before had worn the confident look of someone who knows that he can open a bottle of *acqua minerale* with a flourish worthy of a symphonic cymbalist. He walks back to the bar, where ice cream dishes are being prepared as they have been prepared since 1720, and shakes his head. He says, "*La signora diche no e riuscito*," or words to that effect.

"*La signora?*" the *tartufo* maker says.

The waiter nods toward our table. "*La princi-pessa*," he says.

The *tartufo* maker hangs his head. He takes off his apron, folds it neatly on the marble counter, and walks toward the door. He understands that there is nothing left except to apprentice with his sour father-in-law as a Lambretta mechanic. The waiter has torn off his own braided epaulets. The orchestra has switched from a waltz to a dirge. The head-waiter has taken upon himself the sad duty of informing the proprietor what has transpired.

"Not successful?" the proprietor repeats, in four languages.

The headwaiter, a loyal employee, tries to cheer up the proprietor. "Your café is on an awfully nice piazza," he says. "The waiters open bottles with splendid flourishes."

"Not successful," the proprietor says again. Lord Byron and Proust mean nothing. The place has failed inspection.

It did mean close to Veronelli's heart. That was obvious early in the meal at La Villa Miranda, in a village called Radda in Chianti, south of Florence. By that time I knew that what was close to Veronelli's heart was likely to be close to my own — even though I still made occasional errors in translation, such as confusing the weekly closing day with the wine specialty. On the drive to Radda, winding through the vineyards that produce the grapes for Chianti Classico wine, I had one moment of doubt about whether I had understood the heart symbol correctly after all: a highway sign advertising La Villa Miranda showed a vast estate that looked a little like Versailles. For all I know, it was in fact Versailles. It was certainly not La Villa Miranda, which turned out to be a modest building by the side of the road that had the close, woody atmosphere of a country pub.

Miranda herself was there — an ample, jolly woman who presided over everything from the stove to the totting up of the checks. The meal was spectacular. We had salami (*produzione*, it almost goes without saying, *propria*), vegetable soup, ravioli with wild mushrooms, fried potatoes, pigeon cooked according to that secret Tuscan method that transforms it into mostly crunch, and Miranda's own pecorino cheese. As we left, Miranda was taking a break at the table of a diner who had been eating alone, and when she noticed me gazing covetously at a chicken dish the diner was having, she immediately snatched up the plate and insisted that I sample a bit. From the sample I was able to deduce the recipe: a fairy godmother shows up at a McDonald's outlet on a double lane outside of Houston, in-

forms the proprietor that she is going to demonstrate to him what the travesty he sells as Chicken
McNuggets could taste like if prepared by an artist
instead of a plastic factory, waves her wand, gives
the proprietor an exceedingly small bite of what has
magically appeared in the frying pan, and whisks
the rest off to La Villa Miranda.

Veronelli's review had said that among Miranda's
dessert specialties was *gelato di crema*. More than
once, I had heard Alice say, "*Crema* is the real test."
*Crema* is something like vanilla, but because of the
heavy custard base of Italian ice cream, it can taste
like the sort of custard your grandmother used to
make when she was trying to wheedle something
out of your grandfather. In a *trattoria* just off the
*autostrada* outside of Bologna, we had eaten a version that I knew Alice had fastened on as encom-
passing the standards of the breed. We had spent
some time in the area around Florence after that,
looking for the Bologna ideal. Tuscany had not
failed completely. Alice had been impressed with a
place called Gelateria Venato in Lucca. In Siena, a
café in the Piazza del Campo brought a brief smile
to her lips with its pear. She compared the taste of
the chocolate from a little grocery store in the market town of Greve to the taste of homemade chocolate pudding. But Alice had not found what she
might have referred to as *crema bolognese*. I was

hoping that Miranda's *crema* would be it — an indication that the wise Veronelli knew places that could get close to any number of hearts at the same meal. It was not to be. After a spoonful of Miranda's *crema*, Alice appeared to be mildly impressed. But then she said, "Still not Bologna." Even Veronelli has his limitations.

By the time we headed for Rome, after a couple of weeks in Tuscany, Alice's *gelateria* aides-de-camp were more than a couple of steps behind. Sarah, who had pretty much limited herself to chocolate chip from the start, had all but abandoned *gelati* for an ice cream sandwich marketed under the unlikely Italian name of Cooky Snack — by the same company that also produced ice cream novelties called Sport Goofy, Blob, and Bubble O'Bill. I had been poring over my Veronelli without success in an effort to find a restaurant whose specialties might include both the fried artichokes I love to eat in Rome and some distinguished *gelati*. But I was feeling less confident of mastering Veronelli after discovering that the reason he mentioned *parcheggio*, which I had taken to be a type of cheese, after the address of each restaurant was that *parcheggio* means parking.

In Rome, though, Alice seemed to gain energy from the feeling that she was finally among her peers. Particularly around the Pantheon, there are streets in Rome where practically everyone seems to be carrying an ice cream cone. In Rome there are serious disputes among connoisseurs about the relative merits of the slick Gelateria della Palma and the more traditional Giolitti. Alice was in the position of a chess fanatic who, after years of feeling a bit isolated in Newport Beach, suddenly finds himself in Leningrad.

She tried della Palma ("This is serious"). She tried Giolitti ("The chocolate is fabulous, the *nocciola* is fabulous, the *baci* is the best thing I've ever tasted"). She ate the traditional *tartufo* at Tre Scalini in the Piazza Navona. Still, as we got aboard the plane to return to New York, she had some regrets. She had never matched the Bologna *crema*. Having not had a chance to try some of the challengers to Tre Scalini that her touts had suggested, she reminded me, she had eaten only one *tartufo* the entire trip.

"How about the *tartufo* in Venice?" I said.

"That didn't count," she said.

"Apparently some of these *gelaterias* have opened branches in New York," I said.

"It's not the same," she said. "It doesn't travel."

On our next trip, we decided, we would have to head south — perhaps in the direction of Capri, where Alice had once found several *nocciolas* worthy of respect. Veronelli listed a number of restaurants in that area, some of them designated by an ace of clubs (gambling rooms available?). I could imagine us in an outdoor café in Capri. Those who had been observing our roles might point and say, "She eats ice cream. He studies Veronelli and schleps the luggage."

# 14

## Beach Picnic

As THE BOAT FROM ST. THOMAS neared St. John, it occurred to me again that I might have made a serious mistake leaving behind my ham. You could say, after all, that our entire trip had been based on that ham. In our family, the possibility of renting a house for a week on St. John had been kicking around for years; Abigail and Sarah were so strongly for it that I sometimes referred to them as "the St. John lobby." We had been on St. John briefly during the week we'd spent on St. Thomas, only a short ferry ride away. St. Thomas is known mainly for recreational shopping — its principal town, Charlotte Amalie, had already been a tax-free port for a century and a half when the United States bought St. Thomas and St. John and St. Croix from Denmark toward the end of the five or six thousand years of human history now thought of as the pre-credit-card era — and what I remember most vividly about our week there was trying to explain to Abigail and Sarah that the mere existence of a customs exemption of $800 per person does not mean that each person is actually required to spend $800. ("I happen to know of a man who was permitted to leave even though he had purchased only $68.50 worth of goods. He is now living happily in Metuchen, New Jersey.") I was rather intent on getting the point across because according to what I could see from the shopping patterns on St. Thomas, our family would ordinarily have been expected to buy $3,200 worth of perfume — enough perfume, I figured, to neutralize the aroma of a fair-sized cattle feedlot.

What Abigail and Sarah remembered most vividly were rumless piña coladas — it was their first crack at rumless piña coladas — and the spectacular beaches on St. John. The beaches are accessible to everyone through inclusion in the Virgin Islands National Park, which covers nearly three quarters of the island, and, just as important, going to the beach is pretty much all there is to do — a state of affairs that Abigail and Sarah would think of as what ham purveyors call Hog Heaven. We had talked about it a lot, but the conversation usually ended with a simple question: What would we eat?

## Beach Picnic

The question went beyond the dismal food we had come to expect in Virgin Islands restaurants. (On St. Thomas, the restaurants had seemed to specialize in that old Caribbean standby, Miami frozen fish covered with Number 22 sunblock, and my attempts to find some native cooking had resulted mainly in the discovery of bullfoot soup.) In a house on St. John, we would presumably have our own kitchen, but we'd be dependent on the ingredients available in the island stores. Our only previous experience in that line — in the British Virgin Islands, where we had once rented a house when Abigail was a baby — had produced the shopping incident that I have alluded to ever since when the subject of Caribbean eating comes up. On a shopping trip to Roadtown, the capital, Alice ordered a chicken and asked that it be cut up. When we returned from our other errands, we found that the butcher had taken a frozen chicken and run it through a band saw, producing what looked like some grotesque new form of lunchmeat.

The memory of that chicken caused a lot of conversations about St. John rentals to fizzle and die. Then, during one of the conversations, my eye happened to fall on a country ham that was hanging in our living room. Maybe I'd better explain the presence of a ham in our living room; Abigail and Sarah seem to think it requires an explanation whenever they bring friends home for the first time. Now and then, we have arranged to buy a country ham from Kentucky. The ham often arrives with a wire attached to it, and since we have a couple of stalking cats, I put the ham out of their reach by attaching the wire to a living room beam in what seems to be a natural hanging place — a spot where we once briefly considered hanging a philodendron. The first time I hung a ham in the living room, Alice pointed out that some of the people expected at a sort of PTA gathering about to be held at our house didn't know us well enough to see the clear logic involved in the ham's presence, so I put a three-by-five card of the sort used in art galleries on a post next to the ham. The card said, "Country ham. 1983. J. T. Mitchum. Meat and wire composition." Since then, I've found that even without the card many guests tend to take the country ham as a work of art, which, at least in the view of people who have eaten one of Mr. Mitchum's, it is.

Contemplating that ham, I found my resistance to renting a house in St. John melting away. We could take the ham along to sustain us, in the way a band of Plains Indians, living in happier times, would have brought their newly killed buffalo to the next camp site. We would bring other provisions from the neighborhood. We would not be dependent on frozen chicken lunchmeat. We made arrangements to rent a house for a week on St. John.

Then I left the ham at home. Not because it

slipped my mind. A country ham is not the sort of thing you simply forget. Alice had argued that it was terribly heavy, that it was more than we needed, that she didn't feel like making biscuits on St. John (because the American Virgin Islands are U.S. territory, the federal law against eating country ham without biscuits applies). I finally agreed, although I couldn't resist pointing out that the remark about its being more than we needed was directly contradicted by the number of times I've heard people who have just finished off a plateful of country ham and biscuits say, "That's exactly what I needed."

I don't mean we arrived in St. John empty-handed. I had brought along an extra suitcase full of provisions. There were some breakfast necessities — tea and the seven-grain bread that Alice likes in the mornings and, of course, a dozen New York bagels. We also had smoked chicken breasts, a package of a Tuscan grain called farro, a couple of packages of spaghetti, sun-dried tomatoes, a package of pignolia nuts, an Italian salami, several slices of the flat Italian bread called focaccia that a man near our house makes every morning, a jar of olive paste, and what Alice usually refers to as her risotto kit — arborio rice, fresh parmesan cheese, olive oil, wild mushrooms, a head of garlic, a large onion, and a can of chicken broth. Better safe than sorry.

Finding a place to rent had turned out to be relatively simple. St. John is organized on the premise that a lot of visitors will want to rent a house. The only hotels of any size on the island are Caneel Bay, one of the first of the resorts that the Rockefellers built for those who feel the need of being cosseted for a few days in reassuringly conventional luxury, and a new resort called the Virgin Grand, a touch of flash that is always mentioned in the first thirty seconds of any discussion about whether the island is in danger of being ruined by development.

The de facto concierges of St. John are a dozen or so property managers, each of whom presides over a small array of houses that seem to have been built with renting in mind — which is to say that you can usually count on your towels being of a uniform color and you don't have to toss somebody else's teddy bears off the bed to go to sleep. Most of the houses are tacked onto the side of a hill — the side of a hill is about the only place to build a house on St. John, which has so many ups and downs that its old Indian name was probably Place Where You're Always in First Gear — and have decks whose expansive views are measured by how many bays are visible. Our house was a simple but cheery two-bedroom place with what I would call a one-and-a-sliver-bay view. It had a kitchen more than adequate for the preparation of an arrival supper of grilled smoked-chicken sandwiches on focaccia. As I ate one, I tried to keep in mind that out there in the dark somewhere people were probably eating Miami frozen fish with sunblock. We weren't safe yet.

I think it was the phrase "fresh fish" that gave me the first hint that sustaining life on St. John might be easier than I had anticipated. For years, the American Virgin Islands have been known for being surrounded by fish that never seem to make it onto a plate. The first sunny news about fresh fish came accompanied by a small black cloud: local fishermen, I was told, showed up on Tuesday and Thursday mornings on a dock behind the customs shed in Cruz Bay, the one place on St. John that more or less passes as a town, but some of the coral-feeding fish they catch had lately been carrying a disease called ciguatera, which attacks your central nervous system. There was conflicting information around on the subject of ciguatera. I met people in St. John who said that they don't hesitate to eat coral-feeders, and I met someone who said she had been horribly ill from eating one kingfish. I met someone who said that in Japan ciguatera, which isn't detectable by taste or smell, is avoided by putting the fish in a bucket of water with a quarter and discarding it if the quarter tarnishes. I decided to pass. The phrase "attacks your central nervous system" tends to dull my appetite; also, I kept wondering what all those American quarters were doing in Japan.

It turned out, though, that a store in Cruz Bay

called Caribbean Natural Foods sold fresh deep-
water fish like tuna — not to speak of soy sauce and
rice wine and sesame oil for the marinade. Caribbean Natural Foods was one of two or three small
but ambitious food stores that had opened since our
previous visit to St. John, and among them the island had available California wine and Tsingtao
beer and Silver Palate chocolate sauce and Ben &
Jerry's ice cream (including my daughters' favorite
flavor, Dastardly Mash) and New York bagels and
real pastrami and a salad identified as "tortellini
with walnut pesto sauce and sour cream." I suppose
there are old St. John hands who grumble that the
world of exotic beers and gourmet ice cream was
what they were trying to get away from, but there
must be a lot of regular visitors who feel like celebrating the expansion of available foodstuffs with
an appropriately catered parade.

Leading the parade would be people serious about
picnics. On St. John, the pleasantness of beaches
tends to vary roughly in direct proportion to how
hard it is to get there. Anyone who chooses a
beach on St. John because it has a convenient parking lot or a commissary or a marked underwater
trail or plenty of changing rooms may find himself
thinking at some point in the afternoon that he
should have paid more attention to what his mother
said about the rewards that come to those willing to

make a little extra effort. (A difficult road, though, is not an absolute guarantee of peacefulness: someone who has been reading a novel on what seemed like an out-of-the-way beach may look up from his book and find that twenty boats of one sort or another have materialized in a line across the bay, prepared to disgorge a small but expensively outfitted invasion force.) Once you're settled in at the beach, the prospect of going back to Cruz Bay for lunch can provoke the great bicultural moan: "*Quel schlep!*" I don't know what people used to do about lunch at a beach like Francis Bay, where a beach-lounger can watch pelicans as they have a go at the flying fish and a snorkler with a little patience can usually spot a giant sea turtle. By the time we got there, you could reach into the ice chest for a sea-food-salad sandwich and a bottle of Dos Equis.

At Salt Pond, a spectacular beach on the more remote eastern end of the island, we did leave for lunch one day in order to go to Hazel's, where Hazel Eugene, whose wanderings after she left St. Lucia included New Orleans, was said to serve what she sometimes called Caribbean Creole cooking. Hazel's turned out to be on the ground floor of a sort of aqua house that had goats wandering around the back and a neighbor who seemed to be the island's leading collector of auto bodies. Its signs identified it as SEABREEZE: GROCERY, RESTAURANT, BAR, and while we were there Hazel would occasionally leave the kitchen to pour a couple of shots or to fill a shopping list that might consist of a box of Kraft Macaroni & Cheese dinner, a bottle of rum, and a beer for the ride home. She also waited on tables, and in that role she began a lot of sentences with "I could do you . . ." as in "I could do you some of my fried chicken with cottage fries" or "I could do you some codfish fritters and some of my special pumpkin soup to start." Hazel did us all of that, plus some blackened shark and some seafood creole and some puffed shrimp and some chicken curry and a plate of assorted root vegetables that tasted an awful lot better than they sounded or looked. When it was over, I was just about ready to admit that I might have sold St. John short.

I don't mean I regretted bringing along the extra suitcase. Hazel's was too far to drive at night. Places to eat dinner were limited, although at least one restaurant in Cruz Bay, the Lime Inn, had fish from the Caribbean, of all places, and served it grilled, without even a dash of sunblock on the side. And, of course, we had one dress-up evening in the main dining room at Caneel Bay. What was being sold there, I realized, was simulation of membership in the most prominent country club in town — at a cost that might seem considerable but is, I assume, nothing compared to the kick of the real club's annual dues. The food is of the sort that is described by the most enthusiastic members as "not highly seasoned," and the waiters, playing the role of old club retainers, serve it in a manner so true to the rituals of the upper-middle-class past that you even get a little tray of olives and carrot sticks to nibble on while you're waiting for your shrimp cocktail. The night we were there, the menu offered a marinated conch appetizer as the single reminder that we were on an island rather than in one of the better suburbs, and it listed some California wines as the single reminder that we hadn't found ourselves, willy-nilly, in 1954.

All of which means that we often ate dinner at the place with a one-and-a-sliver-bay view — grilled tuna with some pasta on the side, a great meal of spaghetti with garlic and oil and sun-dried tomatoes, and, finally, the fruits of Alice's risotto kit. It occurred to me, as we ate the risotto and talked about risotto in Milan, that behind our shopping there may have been an unconscious desire to create the Italian West Indies. In fact, I informed those at the table, it hadn't been a bad try — although it might have been improved by bringing along a little more focaccia for the picnics.

Back home, we decided that surviving on St. John had been easy enough to merit a return engagement. A few months later we heard that Hazel had

closed her restaurant and taken her talent for Caribbean Creole cooking elsewhere. It was a blow, but
not a blow severe enough to change our minds about
going back. After all, we still had the country ham.

# 15

## Special Occasion

I HAD THOUGHT I might have to pop for Kashmir.
I tried to keep that in mind when I put down the
deposit for one of the hotels that had been booked
for Alice's birthday trip — a swanky joint in Capri
called the Punta Tragara. Otherwise, what the deposit would have brought to mind was the folk
phrase that is thought to have originated when a
New York resident named Mark Singer was asked
about how the wallpapering of his bathroom had
turned out: "It's nice, but all in all I think I would
have rather had a car."

Alice is a serious celebrator of birthdays. Trying
to explain to people the sort of arrangements normally made for one of Alice's birthdays, I usually
have to allude to historical figures for comparison —

Cleopatra, say, or the Shah of Iran. In fact, as we prepared for the birthday in question, it seemed to me that I could still see a faint glow on the distant horizon — perhaps the fires of the outer villages, where the celebrations of the previous birthday were just winding down.

I still run into people now and then who find it surprising that the celebration of Alice's birthday normally requires a week or so. As my father used to say, you meet all kinds. Their surprise often seems to be based on an assumption that a serious celebration of your wife's birthday is old-fashioned, a relic of the days when Jimmy Stewart tried to keep June Allyson happy pretty much through the whole movie. I'm told that times have changed: the New Woman is supposed to be able to fix a carburetor, and the New Couple has a relationship that is modeled not on the relationship between Jimmy Stewart and June Allyson but on the relationship between Butch Cassidy and the Sundance Kid. That misses the point. Taste in celebrating is not based on gender. I suppose it's possible that the Sundance Kid didn't like to make much of his birthdays — they may have struck him as just another reminder that his draw was getting slower by the year — but what if he truly liked a major celebration? What if he looked forward every year to marking the day of his birth with what they used to call in the West "a real wingding, with pink balloons and few survivors"? I think Butch Cassidy would have arranged it. Butch and Sundance were pals. What are pals for?

As it happens, Alice truly likes a major celebration. Also, the birthday in question was what Alice called a "special birthday" — not that I can think of any of Alice's birthday celebrations that I'd describe as off-the-rack. Alice was about to be fifty — what I suppose you could call a half century, although that was not a term we used regularly around the house.

That's why I thought I might have to pop for Kashmir. Alice had often talked about what a gorgeous place Kashmir must be. For a special birthday of the half-century variety, I would obviously have been willing to go to Kashmir, even though it's well known that I hate scenery. The sacrifice could have been one of the presents. I'd just have to figure out a way to wrap it.

I suppose there are only two choices for a special-birthday trip: a place you've always wanted to go or a place you've particularly loved. The decision to go to some places in Italy Alice had particularly loved came about mainly because of Tony and Mary Mackintosh. Tony and Alice were born the same week, and on their fortieth birthdays we had all met in France for a special-birthday trip that I suppose could be described most succinctly as an attempt to see how many celebratory places to eat could be found between Paris and the Mediterranean.

Tony and Mary were interested in celebrating what would be a combined century, and they suggested a trip to Italy that would begin with a visit to a garden an hour or so south of Rome called Ninfa. Alice and I had never heard of Ninfa — although I should point out, just for the record, that I was familiar with a Mexican restaurant by that name in Houston. As it happens, I don't know many gardens by name. In fact, I don't know many flowers by name. Because of that, I've always referred to all flowers as marigolds. Marigold sounds like a flower, and it's easy to spell.

Alice knows a lot of flowers by name. So does Mary. So does Tony. They all love gardens. I wouldn't say that I'm opposed to gardens; it just would never occur to me to go to Italy to see one. On the other hand, it wasn't my birthday. I suppose if we decided to celebrate a special birthday of mine by taking the sort of trip that it would never have occurred to Alice to take — say, a trip the tour packagers might have called Renowned Neighborhood Taverns of the Industrial Midwest — she would have gone along cheerfully. At least, she would have gone along.

"You want to go to a garden in Italy for your birthday?" I asked Alice, just to make sure.

"Yes," Alice said. "I'm not quite ready for Kashmir. Maybe when I'm older."

"Well," I said, getting right into the celebratory spirit of things, "it'll be cheaper than Kashmir."

❦

Maybe. Maybe not. Mary and Tony took charge of scheduling a visit to Ninfa — it's open only one weekend a month unless special arrangements are made in advance — and Alice planned the rest of the trip. That's how I happened to be putting down a deposit at the Punta Tragara — a place that specializes in suites whose terraces overlook the Faraglioni, the huge rocks that jut out of the sea just off the southeastern tip of Capri. The Punta Tragara is what is known in our family as a *principessa* hotel. Although I had begun referring to Alice by royal title in hotels as a way to improve the service ("The drain in our bathtub is a bit too slow to please the *principessa*"), the phrase *"principessa* hotel" had evolved into a way to describe the sort of hotel that is fit for authentic princesses — particularly those married to Arab oil sheiks. The San Domenico, in Taormina, where we had once spent a few days with Tony and Mary, was, we all agreed, properly described as a *principessa* hotel, partly because having your shirts washed there costs so much that I framed the laundry bill.

The plan was to follow a visit to Ninfa with a few days at the Punta Tragara and a couple of days at the San Pietro — another *principessa* hotel, just outside Positano. The *principessa* phase of the trip would be followed by what I thought of as the *contessa* phase: five or six days in a Tuscan farmhouse some friends of ours had lent us in the Chianti Classico wine country just north of Siena. On birthday trips, it is not Alice's custom to travel as a commoner.

All of this, of course, was predicated on the fact that Alice was born in May. I don't mean to put this forward as an extra wrinkle on modern family planning, but if someone is going to turn out to be a serious celebrator of birthdays, May is a good month for being born. I can't imagine Alice as someone born in February. May is a perfect time for Italian *principessa* hotels: it's warm enough to swim but often so uncrowded that it's easy to consider the place part of your own royal holdings. May is a perfect time to be in Tuscany — a time when it's still not too hot for a *contessa* to spend some time next to the pool, gazing approvingly over the vineyards that surround her. It's a perfect time to drive through the countryside or wander through a market.

In fact, when we landed in Rome, we went straight to the market in the Campo di Fiori, where one of the vendors showed us how to break open a fruit we had never seen before — something he called a *mangostana*, which has mild but delicious pods that look like peeled garlic cloves. Looking around at the profusion in the Campo di Fiori, Alice said May would certainly be a perfect time to see the garden at Ninfa. An old tune about all of that began to run through my head, but I couldn't remember the words. Something like "The marigolds bloom in the spring, tra-la, the marigolds bloom in the spring."

I was so pleased to see Tony and Mary that I almost forgave Mary for presenting to Alice, as a birthday gift, a large coffee-table book called *Gardens of the Italian Villas*, a book that provided Alice with all sorts of ideas about other gardens that didn't look as if they could possibly be missed. I didn't complain openly — the role of a *principessa*'s consort is traditionally to remain in the background — but it occurred to me that we might be in danger of embarking on a garden tour of Italy.

Ninfa was, of course, in the book — described as "perhaps the quintessential romantic garden." Apparently, Ninfa was a thriving town from the late eighth century to the fourteenth century — a place where a pope, Alexander II, was crowned while seeking refuge from a murderous type who claimed to be the pope himself. Toward the end of that period, in 1297, the town was bought by the Caetani family, which held on to it for nearly seven hundred years. Even in Italy that's considered a long run, although for much of that time the place amounted to ruins and swamps that probably wouldn't have been of much interest to anyone else. Finally, in this century, one Caetani began to reclaim the land, and his sister-in-law, a woman from Boston, began planting flowers amidst the ruins. Her daughter took over, and eventually the Caetanis had something appropriate for a full-century-of-birthday celebration.

It feels more like a park than a garden. Even though it's intricately planned, the flowers aren't in formal beds. The Caetanis took the approach to gardening that another distinguished Italian family, the DiMaggios of San Francisco, took to baseball — make it all look natural. Ninfa is a twenty-acre patch of land with meadows and trees and ruins and a river and what seem to be natural growths of flowers that don't grow naturally. Alice and Mary and Tony began emitting garden exclamations — "Will you look at those columbines!" and "Here come the hollyhocks!" and "I've never seen roses climbing up a cypress like that!" — almost as soon as we began our stroll down one of Ninfa's paths.

"Have you ever seen calla lilies that just seem to be growing wild in the woods that way?" one of them said.

"To the best of my knowledge, I've never seen a calla lily," I replied.

I see only marigolds, of course. I must admit, though, that I'd never seen them in such profusion, in such a setting — marigolds climbing up the ruins of a wall, meadows of marigolds, water marigolds floating next to a Roman bridge, a weeping marigold tree standing framed in an ancient arch.

Alice said it was the best garden she had ever seen.

"Absolutely," I said. "Any garden we went to after this would just be an anticlimax."

In Capri it occurred to me that Alice might be under the impression that, in the way that the twenty-fifth anniversary is traditionally a time for silver, the fiftieth birthday is traditionally a time for flowers. She and Mary were standing on the terrace of the Mackintoshes' suite, deadheading some flowers that looked to me like marigolds while discussing whether Caprisian lobelia would survive in a harsher climate.

"I'm sure the hotel appreciates this," I said. "They usually can't find gardeners who will pay them quite this much an hour."

Capri in May was everything the *principessa* had remembered — perfect weather and, of course, a profusion of flowers. There seemed to be fewer day-trippers than I remembered from our previous visit in May, and fewer of the street photographers who back-pedal in front of strolling visitors in the evening with flashbulbs flashing, making a simple tourist feel like an internationally famous movie star or someone who has just been indicted for insider trading. One of the things Alice loves about Capri is that, on a large part of the island, it is Italy without cars or motorcycles — that rare refuge where a romantic supper at a sidewalk restaurant cannot include the discovery that a passing Vespa has garnished your salad with exhaust fumes. I have to admit that except for the oppressive presence of a spectacular view everywhere you look, I like Capri in May myself. On this trip, in fact, I realized that, difficult as it would be for an August day-tripper to believe, Capri in May was the rough model for my fantasy of that sunny island of Santo Prosciutto, I.W.I., where the chef hums an aria while he grills your *langostina* and the waiter handles the wine question with an eloquent "You won raid or whyut?"

Positano was also everything Alice had remembered; the last time we were there, nine years before, she had decided it was better as a view than as a town. A perfect view of Positano climbing up from the Gulf of Salerno is one of the amenities offered by the San Pietro, which is built into the side of a mountain a few miles down the coast — although Alice seemed a bit distracted the first time we took in the view from the terrace of our room. Then I noticed her eyeing the terrace's flower beds. "These geraniums need work," Alice said.

"Well, this is a hotel that caters to your every need," I said. "I could call down to the desk and say, 'The *principessa* requests a trowel.' "

Once Alice had the terrace flowers in shape, we were free to do some of the things she remembered having loved before. We made our way along the Amalfi Drive to Vietri and picked through the pottery in a factory where nine years before we had bought, for something like a dollar apiece, some brightly painted soup bowls that turned out to say on the bottom MADE EXPRESSLY FOR GUMP'S, SAN FRANCISCO. (While I was trying to negotiate the road to Vietri — missing motorcyclists now and then by six or eight inches, screeching to a halt when a tour bus suddenly loomed up from around a curve — I realized why Alice had fonder memories of the trip than I had. Everybody always describes the Amalfi Drive as having been cut into the mountains high above the Mediterranean. What they don't tell you is that it hasn't been cut very far into the mountains.) We went to Ravello, a few miles inland, for lunch in its dignified old hotel and a stroll through a garden that had been mentioned in the garden book. It was a conventional garden, and Alice said that after Ninfa it was a letdown.

"Don't worry," I said. "Tuscany will be alive with marigolds."

❧

It was. There were wild red marigolds in the vineyards. As a special gift, our hostess had left an elaborate, carefully planned garden, with serious instructions for watering and upkeep. Even aside from the profusion of marigolds, Tuscany measured up to Alice's expectations. The house was perfect — a simply and beautifully done-up stone farmhouse with a swimming pool and views of vineyards in every direction. The food was the Tuscan food that Alice loves — particularly the grilled *porcini* mushrooms that come the size of smallish steaks. I spent a lot of my time seeking out restaurants that had *ribollita*, a sort of soupless minestrone soup made with vegetables and bread. It wasn't my birthday, of course, but even the help have to keep their strength up. Alice spent a lot of her time as a *contessa* — reading next to the pool, gazing over the vineyards, bestowing approval on the lunch salads that were brought to her from a world-class take-out deli I found near the Campo in Siena.

But then it was over. We were back in Rome, scheduled to take a plane home the next morning. Tony and Mary had already gone back to London. Alice's birthday trip had lasted only two weeks —

plus, of course, a week of celebration in New York before we left. Alice and I were in the Campo di Fiori, looking around for some airplane-picnic supplies, when I reminded her that, to put it in military terms, I would soon be taken off my temporary-duty assignment to the birthday-celebration unit and reassigned to my regular duties. Alice said she thought she could manage the transition to life as an ordinary citizen. Just then we reached the stand where we had tried a *mangostana* a couple of weeks before, and decided to have one for the road. The same vendor picked one out for us, but when I reached for my wallet, he held up his hand and shook his head. He handed the fruit to Alice, with a smile and a slight bow. "*Omaggio*," he said. The word means not just "homage" but also "complimentary offering." Either way, it must be the sort of gesture that's made to *principessas* and *contessas* all the time.